Saffron Barker Vs. Real Life

Sally B xo

Saffron Barker

with Jordan Paramor

SAFFRON BARKER VS. REAL LIFE

My perfectly filtered life

(Sort of. But not really at all)

HODDER & STOUGHTON

First published in Great Britain in 2017 by Hodder & Stoughton
An Hachette UK Company

1

Line illustrations by Saffron Stocker

A CIP catalogue record for this title is available from the British Library

ISBN 978 1 473 66582 8
eBook ISBN 978 1 473 66584 2

Typeset in Celeste by Palimpsest Book Production Limited,
Falkirk, Stirlingshire
Printed and bound in Great Britain by Clays Ltd, St Ives plc

Hodder & Stoughton policy is to use papers that are natural, renewable and recyclable products and made from wood grown in sustainable forests. The logging and manufacturing processes are expected to conform to the environmental regulations of the country of origin.

Hodder & Stoughton Ltd
Carmelite House
50 Victoria Embankment
London EC4Y 0DZ

www.hodder.co.uk

This book is for my incredible family, friends and subscribers, who are always there for me.

INTRODUCTION

I've written a book! About my life! And about a completely imaginary life I made up in my head! I really hope you all enjoy it. You guys are literally the best. If it wasn't for you, I wouldn't be having the most fun vlogging, roping my friends and family into crazy challenges, and living the life of my dreams.

My life may not always be perfect, but in my opinion it's pretty amazing. Fails and all. And you're going to hear <all> about those . . .

Loads of love,
Saffron xxx

CHAPTER 1

January

January 1st – My Real Life

Happy New Year everyone! It's a whole new year, which means it's time to make lots of resolutions I'm not going to keep.

No wait, this year will be different. This year, I'm going to stick to them and by February I'll be a new woman. Well, girl.

I've set myself loads of goals that are going to change my life. I'm going to get healthier, go to the gym, stop eating cereal for dinner, clear out my wardrobe, stop buying things I don't need, be nicer to my little brother Jed – you name it.

This year, I want to travel more and do more charity work.

I also want to get my viewers up to a magic number I've got in my head, and post a vlog every single day.

My mum has asked me to set a goal to clean my room, but that's never going to happen. She's also asked me to stop arguing with my brothers, but that's another promise I just can't keep. I think it's important to manage expectations.

New Year's Day is always kind of tough, and for some reason I think I'm magically going to wake up a new person with the strength and stamina of an Olympic athlete.

I kind of <forced> myself to start my health kick on the 2nd because we always go out for dinner as a family on the

1st, and no one wants to be gazing at the menu trying to choose the healthiest option when all you want is chips. And maybe some cake.

So instead of going to the gym I'll buy some new gym gear because that will motivate me and I'll be READY FOR IT. I'll have new presents and a new attitude, and I'll know that this year I'm going to be a #winner

Every year I say I'm going to stop biting my nails. This was the first year I didn't have to make that deal with myself, because I've got extensions now.

Amazingly, I still manage to bite those off, even though it's supposed to be impossible, but at least my nails look better than they used to. They were shocking. Really short and split and horrible. At times, they were so chewed up and they'd have dents in them.

(Casey: 'You have got the nails of a small boy.')

I get my nails done once every two weeks now, but sometimes I have to go to the salon earlier because I've chewed a couple of the extensions off. It's so bad.

A new year always makes me think about life and where mine is going. You know, what I'm doing and what I need to change to get where I want to be. All that stuff slightly hurts my head, but we all have to do it.

How I win at life

- ★ Being confident.
- ★ Being happy.
- ★ Staying positive.
- ★ Being grateful for everything that happens.
- ★ Being excited about what could happen every single day.
- ★ Not worrying about what other people are doing.

SIDE NOTE: I genuinely think you can't win at life if you're always comparing yourself to other people. Compare-itis does nothing but make you miserable. And if you're jealous of people, it does you no favours. All it does is bring you down. Be happy for other people. That's a massive #win

When you're happy it shines out of you. When you're angry or bitter or jealous, that shows through too. That's the easiest way to #fail

What I'd really like to win at and don't

- ★ Photoshop.
- ★ Spelling.
- ★ Having nicer feet.

January 3rd

January is officially miserable. The weather is <gross>, and when I look out the window all I want to do is lie on the sofa covered with a giant blanket and stay there for a few days while my mum passes me food. Usually by January 3rd I've broken half my resolutions and my motivation has gone. This sucks.

This year was worse than usual because technically I was still recovering from a pretty terrible break-up. I felt a bit 'blah' about things, but then I gave myself a kick up the backside and realized I can do whatever I choose, and feel however I want. And I chose to create an amazing fantasy life, right here, right now.

Who says we can only live one life? I want two. And in my other one, I'm living in LA, where it's always sunny and the guys love British girls more than anything else in the world. Let's do this!

January 1st – My fantasy life

Forget eating cake and crying at romantic movies, sometimes the only way to get over a bad break-up is to go out and become the biggest, most kick-ass YouTuber on the planet and take over the world. And this year, that's exactly what I'm going to do. Watch out LA – I'm coming to get you!

Yes, that's right, I'm going to squeeze every single bit of clothing I own into a suitcase, fill another one with make-up, camera equipment and my Hello Kitty teddy (I've had her since I was a baby and she goes everywhere with me), and prepare to head off to Hollywood to dine at The Nice Guy and become best friends with Kendall and Kylie. And you're coming with me.

Anyone who knows me knows I'm the worst packer in the world. I try and pack everything I own. Then I have to repack, and only end up taking, like, two things out. If my passport wasn't essential, I would end up leaving it at home because it would mean I could squeeze in some more earrings. I always think if you're taking a case, you may as well fill it up.

A friend of mine called Anastasia came to stay recently and she had everything in one handbag. A handbag! For four days! I wouldn't even have fitted my make-up in the bag. I was so shocked.

My mum's best packing tip is to put all your jewellery in your hand luggage when you're going away, because it's the thing that weighs the most. It makes sense because no one wants to pay the crazy fees when their bag is too heavy. But your shoulder does really ache after a while.

January 4th

I'm at the airport, ya'll! Saying goodbye to my family was super sad. They all came to wave me off and I didn't stop crying until I got to duty-free. The sight of all that bargain MAC is enough to put a smile back on anyone's face.

Three lipsticks and an eye-shadow palette later (the Solar Glow Times Nine, since you ask – it's, like, so pretty and will look amazing with the golden tan I'll have by this time next week), and I'm heading to my beloved Nando's for a farewell meal.

I can't believe I'm going to be without it for so long. Seriously, how is there not one in LA yet? Come on, Nando's! If I'm going to be there for at least a year (maybe longer, if I fall in love with it and never want to leave), I need my home comforts.

I've got my Beats on, I'm listening to some Flo Rida and I'm ready for the next phase of my life. Bring. It. On.

But first, I've got to run to the gate because they're calling my name. I haven't even finished my chips. WAH!

My family and I are always the ones whose names are being called out over the tannoy when the airline is waiting for everyone to board. We're that family who are running to the gate while the announcer is saying, 'Last call for Barker'.

We're usually shopping or eating and we lose track of time, which is very easy when there's so much good stuff to buy!

To be fair, airports are really confusing. You always think your departure gate is going to be five minutes away and then it's, like, an hour's walk. The worst airport for that is Amsterdam. I'm not joking; it took me about an hour to get to a gate there once. I felt like I should have been awarded a medal at the end of it.

The things I always take with me on a flight are an eye mask, a notepad and pen, ear plugs, a travel pillow, earphones, my laptop, sweets, moisturizer, perfume (in case I've got someone smelly next to me) and fluffy socks. My hand luggage is usually quite bulky, but it's worth it.

I really enjoy flying, and I really, <really> love it when I get upgraded, which has happened to me a few times. The only problem is that once you've flown in total luxury, it's so hard to go back to economy. I almost wish I'd never experienced first class, because it is literally the best thing ever. You get given pyjamas and TVs and beds to chill in. I didn't want the flight to end the first time I got an upgrade. I felt like a proper princess.

I'm desperate to fly Emirates first class but it's over £10,000 a ticket! You get your own bedroom with a shower and everything, but to be honest I'd want my own plane for that money. How ridiculous is that? And how gutted would you be if you fell asleep for the entire journey and missed all your meals and your free spa treatments? I'd probably drink a load of coffee, even though I don't like it, just to stay awake.

I'm really lucky because even though I've been on a few bad flights, I don't get scared of turbulence. My mum said that when us kids were young we went on a really rough flight, and instead of being afraid we started whooping and waving our arms around like we were on a roller-coaster. I bet that wasn't at all annoying for the other passengers.

The worst thing that's happened to me on a flight was when I got sat next to a man who smelt really bad. I know that's horrible, but he did. Every time he moved in his seat I got a whiff of it, hence I always carry perfume with me now. I ended up having to buy some perfume from the plane's duty-free, and whenever he went to the loo I sprayed it on his seat. Now I can't use that perfume, because it always reminds me of him. It's almost a worse smell than the man himself. If I walk past someone who's wearing that fragrance I just <know>. It's actually such a nice smell, but now all I think of is man sweat.

Another time I was on a flight and, being very clumsy, I spilt a bright-red drink on my clean, white Converse and they looked ridiculous. They were more red than white, and it looked like I'd got air sickness and thrown up on them. So cringe.

So, I've landed in LA and it's so cool. I'm staying with a friend called Leonie, who's a fellow YouTuber. Only I can't find her. LAX is huge! But I already feel really glamorous. I've been to LA before and had a wicked time, but now I've got my work

visa and I'm going to be lunching like an A-lister and partying like a rapper.

Completely random link: Now I've talked about my first upgrade, here are some more of my firsts (I told you it was random):

The first celeb I ever met
Zoella and Alfie. I'd been watching them online for about six months and I saw them when I was shopping in Brighton one day. I was so excited, I went over and got a picture of them and they were so nice about it. It's so weird that now people do that to me!

Zoella once tweeted me about my girl band, Born2Blush, and said she wanted to come and see us, and it was the best thing that had ever happened to us. Me and the other girls were amazed. They actually recognized me from the girl band that day in Brighton, and I was <buzzing>.

My first job
One summer, my friend Jazmine and I decided we wanted to earn some money, but we weren't old enough to get a proper job so we decided to set up a babysitting and cleaning

business. We made our own cards on the computers at school and we handed them out to people we knew.

We babysat Jazmine's auntie's two little kids and we got £10 for two hours. It was the best thing, but we ended up spending the money on loads of treats to keep the kids quiet the next time we looked after them.

Jazmine is a saver but I can't save, so I spent any money I had left over on make-up. I'm definitely a spender when it comes to money. I've never got money in my purse, because as soon as it's in there, it's gone again. I could never save up and buy something at the end of the week. If I want something, I want it there and then. I'm also really impulsive. I might be desperate to buy something and be dreaming about getting it for ages, but then if I see something else, I'll end up buying that instead because I get overexcited. Then I'll be furious that I don't have enough money for what I originally wanted 👎.

My best money tip would be to not be like me. I'm impatient. I've tried to save up for things in the past but I haven't lasted. The most expensive things I've ever bought are my Apple Mac and my cameras.

I love doing car-boot sales to make money because I find them really satisfying, and I used to sell stuff on eBay if I needed extra cash. But it's one of those things I never seem to get round to doing now. I'll get a collection of stuff together and have it all ready to go, and then six months later it's still sat in a cupboard waiting to be sold, and I end up giving it away instead.

My first solo shopping trip

Before I hit Year Nine, I hated shopping. I know. It feels crazy writing those words. Mum would make me go with her and I'd want to cry. Then one day, I went out to town with some of my friends and one of them was a proper shopaholic and she showed me the way!

She always had nice handbags and I decided to buy my first ever one, from Cath Kidston. It was a beige, flowery number and it cost about £35. I'd never spent as much as that on one thing before, and I was in shock for ages because it felt like <so> much money.

I brought it home and showed it to my mum, and she was so proud of me. I used it for the next couple of years and I think I've still got it in my room somewhere. Unless my mum has given it to the charity shop, which is a thing she does . . .

My first meal out with my mates

Because I'm so fussy about food, I'd always claimed to hate Nando's and I refused to go. I thought it was going to be spicy and would burn my mouth. Then I went with some friends for our first meal out without our parents and realized I loved it. Now I go about four times a week, which is ridiculous. Once I'd tasted Nando's chicken, there was no going back.

The first book I ever read
I read every single *Daisy and the Trouble with . . .* book by Kes Grey. They are the best ever. I actually would read them again now. I realized recently there was a new one and I've got to get it to see what Daisy is up to now.

The first film I ever watched
I saw *Pooh's Heffalump Movie* when I was four but I don't remember it at all, so I need to re-watch it. I still love Disney. I defy <anyone> to not love Disney.

January 5th

I'm HEEEEERE! I'm in Leonie's apartment, and she's got a pool, and it's so big, and it's so cool, and I saw someone who might possibly have been someone really famous yesterday, and I can't wait to go and sunbathe, and I've already seen some shops I want to go to, and Leonie and I are going to go out to a swag restaurant this evening and . . . Breathe! OMG! My life is AMAZING!

Leonie is so cool. She's twenty, but she's so sophisticated that she seems older. She's planning to be a fashion designer so most of her YouTube videos are about her designs, and she even makes her own clothes in the apartment.

Leonie always looks so good. Her wardrobe is like heaven with doors. She let me have a look through it yesterday and I could have stolen everything. Her style is everything.

She's also absolutely gorgeous. She's got really long, dark hair and olive skin and the only make-up she wears is winged liner, mascara and a red lip. Her favourite is MAC's Ruby Woo, and it's the perfect shade for her. Her best friend, Beth, picked it out for her because she's a make-up artist. She's going to introduce me to Beth soon and I can't wait, because Leonie said we're really alike and we'll get on so well.

Leonie is going to make me some clothes when she has time, and I'll probably wear them to some really cool events. She's always getting invited to vlogger parties and she got to meet Dylan Sprouse at an event last week. Imagine if I turn up to something and Melissa McCarthy was there? I think I would literally die.

January 14th

Hey guys, sorry it's been so long since I've written but LA has literally been a whirlwind since I got here. Especially because I've been busy looking out for famous people. I saw Cara Delevingne in a juice bar the other day, and I also saw a girl who I'm certain I saw in a photo with Kim Kardashian on Instagram once.

Oh, and did I mention I've met a guy and he's incredible? Like, <incredible>?

Leonie and I were in this totally cool coffee shop called Verve, on Melrose, and this guy walked in and I swear down I thought he was Zac Efron. He was so good-looking, I was worried my eyes were going to fall out.

He came over and started chatting to us – the guys in LA are so much more upfront – and he asked me out on a date. Right there and then! Our conversation went like this:

Him: 'Hi, I'm Ryan.'

(I giggle.)

Him: 'How are you guys doing today?'

(I giggle. Must. Say. Something.)

'Are you just hanging out?'

(I nod. Oh god, I feel so shy. He's too handsome. Please say something, Leonie! I look at her desperately . . .)

Leonie: 'Hi, I'm Leonie and this is my friend, Saffron. She's British.'

Him: 'Oh cool, I love the British.'

(I told you!)

Him: 'Have you been over here long?'

Me: 'No!'

(More nervous laughter. This is not going well.)

Leonie: 'Why don't you sit down with us? We're going to be here for a while.'

Thank <god> for Leonie. It takes a lot for me to be shocked into silence, but I cannot tell you how good looking Ryan is. He's got that kind of olive skin that goes an amazing colour any time he even looks at the sun, his eyes are so blue he looks like he should be in an advert for coloured contact lenses (only they're real), and every time he ruffles his brown, sun-kissed hair, it falls perfectly into place above his amazing eyebrows (I've got serious eyebrow envy right now). Oh yeah, and did I mention he's a model? LA <rocks>.

We all chatted for ages, and when he was talking to me he looked so deeply into my eyes I wondered if he could see my brain (that was supposed to sound romantic or something). He made it very clear he was interested in me, which is totally cool because Leonie isn't looking for a boyfriend right now anyway.

Anyway, I'm seeing Ryan in a couple of days. He's taking

me to Venice Beach to show me around and I can't <wait>. I haven't given my ex a second thought. Moving out here is the best thing I've ever done, and I've only been here for ten days.

The partying hasn't been going as well as I hoped, mainly because I can't get into any of the really hip places over here because of my age. They're super strict. It's not like I want to go and drink or anything, I just want to hang out, but the bouncers are <not> friendly. But it's cool, because Leonie and I are going to Disneyland tomorrow. Yay!

January 15th

Disney is <the best>. Leonie and I ran around wearing sequined Minnie Mouse ears, and we got FastPasses so we didn't have to queue for any of the rides. We felt like proper VIPs, and I lost count of the number of ice creams I ate.

Leonie is so much fun to hang out with. I do miss my friends from home, but we're messaging all the time. Everyone here is so friendly, and I've got some meetings booked in to talk about some potential work projects and – excitement overload – a film role. I'd also like to do some more singing one day. I like the idea of being a top pop star like Katy Perry. I'll probably make my first video in the Bahamas or something.

Tomorrow is my first date with Ryan, and I'm having a

wardrobe meltdown. I bought a gorgeous new pink Bardot top the other day and I'll probably just wear it with some ripped jeans, but I have no idea about my shoes. I want to wear some wedges, but they're probably not great for walking along a beach in? I don't want to wear full-on sandals or flip-flops because I hate my feet and I don't want to put Ryan off (I'm deadly serious), but it will be too hot for trainers. Dilemma!

We've all got disgusting feet in my family. We haven't even got toenails. They're miniature. The nails on my baby toes are so small they're barely even worth varnishing. I swear, I went for a shellac pedicure once and the beautician said she had to concentrate really hard to get the polish on, because you can barely see them. The shame!

I think my toes are really short and stubby, and if anyone takes a photo of me and gets my feet in I hate it. Even if it's just one toe, I ask them to crop them out.

One of the weirdest things I've ever done is have one of those fish pedicure things. It's so strange. It really tickled my feet and I actually felt bad that the poor fish had to eat the skin from my awful feet!

I went to a couple of advert castings when I was a kid. I

didn't know what they were beforehand and both were big old fails.

The first one was for some new children's trainers. I had to bend down and do them up on camera. Even then I had the worst, most chewed nails in the world and when they zoomed in on my hands, it was all over.

The next casting was for flips-flops, so you can imagine how that went with my feet. The casting director probably thought, 'Why have they sent along this girl with these awful toes to try and model sandals?' It was not ideal.

January 16th

If they gave out Oscars for the best date, they would probably create a special award for today's. Ryan is literally amazing. We went to Venice Beach, and he took me to watch all the guys working out on Muscle Beach. Then I got my fortune told by a lady who was sat on the promenade.

I actually did do this once, on Brighton Pier. I went to see a psychic who was in this really dark, caravan-type thing, and she told me to sit down and she started looking into a crystal ball (I swear it was like something out of the olden days).

She asked what I did for a living, and I was really vague and told her I worked with cameras so I didn't give too much away. She told me I was going to be a cameraman one day. Eh?

The most embarrassing thing was that my ex was with me at the time and she told me I was going to marry him. Total cringe! To be honest, at that point I probably thought that too. I thought we were 100 per cent going to be together forever. My mum said I might change my mind when I got older, but I thought she was mad. In my mind, he was perfect and we got on so well. We never stopped laughing and I always felt really safe when I was with him, if that makes sense?

We totally got each other. From the minute we met on a trip to Austria, I knew I kind of liked him. Then we got together later on down the line through social media. We went away together loads and, even though things didn't work out, those will always be some of my favourite memories.

Just because you break up with someone, it doesn't mean

all those good times you had together disappear. They don't suddenly get sucked into this break-up void and not matter anymore. It doesn't matter what happened when you split and how bad (or even good, sometimes!) it was, it doesn't mean you have to hate everything about someone.

(We'll come on to my break-up in more detail later on in the book, because it was a really horrible one, but I will still always be grateful for all the good times we had.)

The fortune teller had some tarot cards, and she asked me to shuffle the pack and then lay them out on the small table in front of us. The table was covered with a couple of patterned scarves like my nan would wear, and as she turned each card over she kept smiling at me and Ryan. I got all embarrassed, and she said she could see love and bright lights in my future, so maybe it meant that Ryan and I were going to get married with loads of fairy lights around us. Or maybe I was getting carried away a bit.

Ryan took me for dinner in this really cute diner, but I was too nervous to eat. Partly because I was worried he'd look under the table and see my feet close up. I'd had to wear sandals because it was so hot and, even though they were really cute, they didn't hide nearly enough of my stunted toes.

When it came to saying goodbye at the end of the night, I so didn't want to go. It had been the most perfect day ever, and Ryan had somehow got more handsome as the day went on. I swear he also got more tanned just from walking around on the beach for an hour, while all I got was a really red nose.

I think it's fair to say I am not a master sunbather. I've only got two colours – white or red. I look like a Drumstick lolly when I've been trying to get a tan for a couple of days.

People always think I'm quite olive-skinned, but I have such pale skin naturally, so I'm always having spray tans. I have to be away for about three or four weeks before I start to go in any way brown and then, as soon as I do, I peel and it all comes off again. What. Is. The. Point? The only time I've had a good tan is when we went to Florida for three weeks and even then I had to really work at it. Sunbathing shouldn't be a chore, but it's so dull I feel like someone should be paying me to do it. I don't even really enjoy sunbathing. I get so bored lying there doing nothing.

My friend Gee sometimes comes on holiday, and she has the most amazing olive skin. I can literally watch her turn brown in a day, while I'm still the colour of one of those squashy shrimp sweets and my nose starts glowing. Even if the rest of me doesn't catch the sun and I've got factor 50 on my nose, I end up looking like Rudolph, which is never a good look.

I usually have a spray tan before I go away on holiday so I look good when I first get my bikini on. But it starts to fade after a few days and my natural luminous-white skin starts to poke through. No word of a lie, I usually go away looking browner than I do when I come back.

When the night came to an end, Ryan hailed me a taxi. As we said goodbye, he leant down to kiss me and I genuinely thought I was going to pass out. How did this happen? How did I meet the most handsome, sexiest and funniest man in the world?

I was so happy in the taxi home, and I ran into the apartment to tell Leonie all about it. I started talking at about 100 miles an hour about my unbelievable day and Leonie kept staring at me.

'Erm, that's all great Saff, but have you looked in the mirror?' she said.

I ran to the bathroom, and I was horrified to see that my usually smudge-proof lipstick had worked its way up towards my nose so I looked like I had a hipster mustache. Noooooooo! I was totally mortified. But on the plus side, at least Ryan had still fancied me enough to kiss me!

I <always> wear lipstick and I feel weird without it. I'm lucky, because lipstick stays on really well on my lips. I can put it on first thing in the morning and it will still be there at night. But I do also have a good technique.

MY FAILSAFE LIPSTICK TRICK

Apply your lipstick, blot it on some tissue, use a brush to sweep on a thin layer of translucent powder, add another layer of lipstick, and it'll last for hours and hours.

January 31th

I can't believe I've nearly done a whole month in LA! It's been the best start to the year I've ever had. I've met so many brilliant new people, the shops here are <beyond>, and I've seen loads of Ryan.

He's so cute and he always messages me when he says he will. There's none of that messing around you get with some boys.

I had that whole emoji dilemma with him to start with, but now I'm pretty relaxed about it! I was the first one to send a heart (a blue one, in case you're interested) and I wasn't sure if he'd send one back, but he totally did. Now it's kind of become our thing.

I've said that he should be in one of my vlogs sometime, but he says he's shy. This from a guy who gets his kit off for a living!

I feel like this has been my really fun month, and next month it's time for the real work to begin. I've got so many things I want to do with my acting and singing, and LA is the best place to do them.

I've been FaceTiming my family literally every night and I know they miss me, and I miss them loads. My mum and I are usually with each other every day, so it feels so weird that she's not here. She will be coming out to visit, but in the meantime I have to make do with sending her 500 messages a day.

Emoji etiquette

In my opinion, there is no such thing as using too many emojis. Some people think I use too many, but I can't text people without them. It feels weird. Now, if I use one and someone doesn't send one back I feel quite offended! I know, it's ridiculous.

One of my friends writes entire messages in emojis, and it takes me hours to work them out because they're so random. It's like she's just hitting the screen and hoping for the best, but it hurts my head. My nan sends loads as well and it's so sweet, but hers make total sense. She gives good emoji.

In my opinion, emojis make things clearer. Like, sometimes you don't know if someone is joking or being serious, but if they send you the laughing emoji, you know they're messing around.

I have had moments where I've sent the wrong emoji at the wrong time. I was texting this guy I know and I sent him two hearts like I would to a friend and, when I realized, I was like, 'Oh no. He's totally going to think I'm flirting with him.'

My ex and I always used to send each other sixteen love hearts every time we messaged. I always used to type them out one by one and it made exactly three rows and it took forever. I assumed he was doing the same, so I couldn't understand how he could reply so quickly. Then I realized he was copying and pasting them. I started doing the same and I didn't want him to know. Then, one day I managed to copy and paste a line of our conversation by mistake as well, and I was so busted.

My favourite emojis are the blue and yellow love hearts, the smiling angel, the peace sign and the tongue and winky face. You can get away with so much using a winky face.

Sometimes the broken heart emoji will say everything when someone is going through a hard time. Emojis are basically amazing.

I won't use the cat emojis because I don't really see the point of them, and I'm not keen on the smirky face. What even is it? It's just really smug and annoying.

The Fam

It's about time I properly introduced you to my family, because the chances are I'll be talking about them a lot in this book. They are my world, honestly. They are just the best people I know.

I had such a great time growing up, and I know how lucky I am. We're like a big gang of mates, really. Of course my parents are my parents when they need to be, but they've always given me loads of freedom and let me go off and do what I want. They knew I didn't want to grow up to be a biologist or a teacher. I always wanted to perform.

So, this is who they are:

Jed – The Sweet One

Jed is my younger brother, and I love him to pieces. Everyone thinks he hates YouTube, but he doesn't really. He watches it all the time and he really enjoys it as a viewer. As a participant? Not so much. He just hates my YouTube and being on camera. Even if I get the back of his head in a shot, he'll moan. But he's getting better.

When I first started doing YouTube, he didn't mind and he was dancing around and joining in, but when he saw the reaction he got from some people when the videos went up, he didn't like it at all and all that stopped.

He actually got loads of love over the internet and everyone thought he was really funny and cute, but he was more bothered about what people said at school, and he found the comments really annoying. I was gearing up to leave school when I first started making videos, but he had another two years to deal with people taking the mickey.

There are only eighteen months between Jed and me, so we did everything together when we were growing up. In fact, a lot of people thought we were twins because we looked quite alike and we've got similar personalities, although he's a bit shyer than I am.

He'll kill me for telling you this, but there are loads of pictures of him in tiaras and fairy wings from when I used to dress him up all the time when he was really young. My mum used to push him round in his buggy wearing one of my princess dresses.

Things kind of changed when I went to high school because I thought I was really grown-up all of a sudden, and it's not very cool to hang out with your younger brother when you're that age. Plus he was, and still is, all about the Xbox, so as soon as he discovered that we didn't spend as much time together.

We went through a stage of arguing a lot a couple of years ago because I was all about the camera. And he really was <not> all about the camera. Thankfully, we argue a lot less now and we've got a pretty good relationship. We take the mickey out of each other, but it's only banter and we never say anything really horrible to each other.He's really kind and he'll do anything for me. Apart from be in my videos, obviously.

Casey – The Cool One

I've always got on well with Casey. I've never been as close to him as I am to Jed, but when I left school we got a lot closer because he's really into YouTube too. So we started hanging out together a lot more and making videos. I think, after not having much in common for so long, that kind of bonded us.

I guess also we were closer in age mentally because I was standing on my own two feet and making my own money. When he realized I was properly growing up, he guided me and helped me out with a lot of things, like how to not spend all my money the minute I got it (I'm still working on that).

He got some hassle from his mates about my YouTubing, but he always stuck up for me and he's always got my back. It also worked well for him because he started doing YouTube off the back of what I was doing. He'd often pop up in my videos and people started commenting that he needed his own channel.

Casey would <love> for me to say he's a cool brother but I find it really hard to get the words out. I guess he is, annoyingly. He's also very headstrong, like me, and once he makes his mind up about things, there's no changing it. I find that <so> annoying at times, but really I'm exactly the same.

Unlike me, Casey really enjoyed school, mainly because he loved sport and he did well in his classes. He's probably the cleverest out of us kids, but I think it's safe to say none of us would give Einstein a run for his money.

Jordan – The Mysterious One

It's so funny, because people are so confused about who Jordan is. People are always talking about him in the comments underneath my videos and trying to find out the deal. Some people think he's my half-brother and some

people think he's my adopted brother, so I'm going to clear it up once and for all so there's no confusion.

Jordan is actually my foster brother. My mum has worked with foster kids for years and a few years ago, when Jordan was in between foster homes, he came and stayed with us. It was only supposed to be temporary but he fitted in so well that he soon became part of the family, and he ended up staying.

He's such a nice guy and, while I consider him to be my brother, we're really close friends too. He's such a lovely guy and he's also always up for a laugh. I'm always roping him into being in my videos! I think sometimes he's a bit like, 'What are you actually making me do?' but he never complains.

I made him watch this video of the YouTube couple Jess and Gabriel once and he cried. It was the sweetest thing. Then I made Casey watch it and he was like, 'Whatever'.

Dad – The Confusing One

My dad is like the funny one of the family, although my mum would disagree and say he's quite stupid. He'll do silly things and not care. People really like him being in my videos because he's got a real character and he's up for anything. I probably got my laid-back, 'don't worry about it' attitude from him.

People think Dad's really funny and lively because he's always really hyper in my videos, but what they don't see is that most nights he sits down and falls asleep on the sofa as soon as he gets in from work. It's like he's two different people. He does work hard though, so it's fair enough.

I think I got my work ethic from him because, even if it's late and I'm really tired, I'll edit videos or reply to messages and do whatever I need to do. I never just kind of leave things and hope for the best. Dad taught me that you can have nice things in life, but they don't just fall into your lap. I got my head around that really early, so I've always been prepared to put in the effort to get the results I want.

Mum – The Best Friend

I feel like my mum kind of shares my life with me because we do everything together, and we always have. We have the biggest laughs and we share a lot. We have this kind of unsaid rule where I borrow her clothes and she borrows my make-up. To be honest, I probably get the better deal because I'm always riffling through her wardrobe, but it kind of balances out.

Mum really helped out when I was in the girl band. Some of her friends thought she was crazy to be so involved, because they didn't understand it. They thought it might blur the lines between her being my mum and helping out with work stuff, but she helps with YouTube too now and it just works. It means so much to me. She's the one who's picked me up when I've felt down and helped me to think positively. She would never try and get me to do anything I don't want to, and she's the one who makes sure I get time to relax and be a normal teenager when things are going a bit crazy.

We're best friends and work buddies, but my mum's my parent first and foremost. One minute we'll be chatting like best mates, and the next she'll be telling me off because I've done something I shouldn't have. She always says being a mum is her most important job, so I just have to suck it up and accept that she's going to put me in my place when I need it. I tell her off when I can get away with it too. I'll be like, 'Mum, you do not need another glass of wine!'

We do get on each other's nerves sometimes and bicker about really stupid things, like most mums and daughters. We still couldn't spend more than two days apart without missing each other though.

Nicole – The One Who Always Has My Back

Nicole is Casey's girlfriend, but we're also super close so she's a good friend too. She's totally a part of our family and I can talk to her about anything. She absolutely adores Casey, but she can really put him in his place if she needs to, and he'll always listen to her.

The other great thing is that if Casey and I argue, more often than not she'll be on my side. Girl's got girl's back!

She's also mum to my first niece, who is literally amazing.

Bella – The Lazy One

Ahhh, Bella is the best thing ever. She's a bichon frise and I love, love, love her, but she is <so> lazy. I love her so much and she's so cute, but she does nothing. <Literally> nothing. All. Day.

She does like going out for walks sometimes, but I'll throw a ball for her and it's like it's a massive effort for her to run over to it, and then she'll never bring it back. She likes being in her bed and being stroked more than anything.

Bella is like one of my best friends and I honestly talk to her all the time when no one is around. I got caught out once when my mum asked who I was talking to the other day, and I was so embarrassed when I had to admit it was Bella Boo. But she's the best listener I know and she never judges me, even when I'm being totally ridiculous.

My cousins – The Amazing Ones

I've got loads of cousins. I honestly lose count! My cousin Callum is a really good mate. He's been in videos and he's always got my back.

My really little cousins, Archie, Ivy, Harvey, Lola and Freddie, all love YouTube and want to be YouTubers, which is adorable.

They're all between four and seven and they record little videos on their iPads. The girls are all so sassy. They're like grown-up women in little bodies. Freddie did my make-up for a video once and it was the most amazing thing you've ever seen. I mean, I looked ridiculous, but she took it really seriously, bless her!

My nan – My Proper Superfan

My nan reads through every single comment on every video I post. Even if there are 10,000 comments on Instagram, she'll read every one. She's subscribed to everything I do and she loves social media. It's how she keeps up with what all of us kids are up to.

She gets notifications so she knows if Casey and I upload a new video. She'll be the first one to leave a comment and she'll reply to other people's comments, even though I tell her not to!

Everyone knows who my nan is and they love her because she's the cutest thing on this planet. Whenever she phones, it takes forever to say goodbye because she has to tell me she loves me about twenty times. I have to start gearing up to finish the conversation about half an hour before I actually need to go!

My granddad – The Secret Superfan

My granddad isn't big on social media. Or so he says. But every now and again he'll mention something he's seen on one of mine or Casey's videos, and he gets totally busted.

I got asked to do a miniseries with TalkTalk, and they wanted one of my parents and one of my grandparents to be in it. My nan wasn't very well so she couldn't do it, and I didn't think in a million years my granddad would say yes. But I asked him and he did!

He came up to London for two days with my mum and me, and we ended up having such a lovely time. He's so funny, because he acts like he's not bothered about it all but he's the first one to congratulate us when something goes well.

And that's just my mum's side of the family! My dad's family is much smaller. It's just my nan and granddad, my auntie and uncle, and my two cousins, Nathan and Sophie.

My Nanny and Granddad Woof Woof – The Animal Lovers
I've called my dad's parents Nanny and Granddad Woof Woof since I was a kid. They had dogs, so that was how I told the difference between them and my other grandparents.

They think it's so funny that I do videos and I don't think they properly understand it, but they always ask me how it's going and I tell them what I've been filming. Maybe I'll get them in a video one day . . .

CHAPTER 2

February

February 1st

It's time! This month is when I start my proper work meetings and I've already got some booked in for tomorrow. Eek.

Some agents have been in contact and said they'd like to represent me because they've seen me in some of Leonie's videos, and they want to launch me properly over here. I've already got quite a lot of American followers, but how cool would it be if I broke America and got invited to go on Ellen, *which is basically how you know you've made it? It's gonna happen.*

February 2nd

So, I met with some agents today and they all want to represent me. I am literally <buzzing>. All I have to do is decide which one I want to go with and then it's fast forward.

There's this one guy called Steve, who is also a film agent, and he represents (or reps, as they call it over here) loads of really big names. When I mentioned I wanted to get into movies, we had this conversation:

Me: 'I would so love to be in some films.'
Steve: 'I'm sure we can make that happen.'
Me: 'Shut. Up.'
Steve: 'Pardon?'
Me: 'Shut. Up.'
Steve: 'Why? What have I said?'
Me: 'Oh no, sorry – it's an expression we say when we're excited about something. I don't <actually> want you to shut up.'
Steve: 'Oh, cool. You <British>.'
Me: 'I know, right?'

Even though things were a bit lost in translation, Steve thinks he may be able to get me some auditions, which would be actually amazing. I'd like to be an action hero. Or Zac Efron's love interest. I don't think that's too much to ask?

I've always loved the idea of acting. I enjoyed drama, but I was never in the school plays because they weren't always the coolest productions to be a part of. They seemed to choose quite lame plays to put on, if I'm being honest.

Instead, I did musical theatre out of school and I got to play Sandy in *Grease* and Dorothy in *The Wizard of Oz.* I also dressed up as Annie once and I looked ridiculous, but I secretly loved it.

I was so into dancing. I started dancing when I was three, and I did competitions everywhere. I had to wear some awful outfits, and when I did line dancing I had to wear sequins and cowboy boots. There's photo evidence somewhere, but my family know what will happen if those pictures ever 'leak'.

I once won a local *X Factor*-type show when I was ten, singing Stevie Wonder's 'I Wish'. Simon Cowell's mum was one of the judges and I won, and an actor called Chris Ellison from an old TV show called *The Bill* gave me my award. <How> random?

I wonder what film sets are like? I'm imagining myself having a massive luxury trailer, with a giant TV and a mini-fridge filled with Diet Coke and chocolate. I'd also have really amazing cushions, and maybe a bed to curl up on in between takes. Putting on a dramatic performance takes a lot of energy.

I'd have a wardrobe with amazing dresses I'd been sent by various designers who are desperate for me to wear their clothes. I'd probably go straight out to red-carpet events from filming so I'd need a good selection of outfits.

And, oh my god, the catering. It would be in-credible. They would have, like, fifty different chicken dishes, because it's my favourite food. And mashed potato would be banned, because even thinking about it makes me feel unwell. I hate it so much. Who invented it? And why?

I hold my hands up and admit I'm a really fussy eater. I basically live on chicken and spend a ridiculous amount of time at Nando's. I'll have plain chicken, corn on the cob and Peri-tamer sauce on the side. I can't have anything hot. I had popcorn chicken in KFC once and it set my mouth on fire. I'm not kidding. I ate a salt and vinegar crisp thinking it was a cheese and onion one once and, on my life, I cried because it burnt my tongue.

I decided to be experimental when I was out for dinner with my family recently, so I tried some noodles and I was so pleased with myself, but I felt like my mouth was on fire. My mum tried my food and said it wasn't even slightly hot, but I think she was faking it because it was <crazily> spicy.

I am aware it's annoying that I'm so fussy about what I put in my mouth but, honestly, if I believed everything I read about food I would never eat anything. Like that rumour that Chicken McNuggets had feathers and feet in them. I mean, ewwwwww. They don't, by the way. Which is a very good thing, because I've eaten them so many times I couldn't even count.

The stupid thing is, I've eaten so many awful things in my videos. I've eaten a fish eyeball, a tarantula and some cow tongue. Oh god, it makes me want to cry just thinking about it. The eyeball popped in my mouth and the middle came out of it, and I had tears streaming down my face. How is that okay? Answer: It's not. I actually went nuts.

I also ate this dish from a Japanese restaurant in Brighton in one of my videos. I didn't know what it was and it smelt of drains. No joke. All I know is that it was something fermented, but other than that I have literally no clue. I can't let myself think about what it could have actually been or I'll cry.

My mum ordered it, and when she went to pick it up even the lady serving her said, 'Are you sure someone wants to eat that?' When Mum got it home and I took the lid off, the smell reminded me of when I used to have to walk past a butcher's shop on the way home from school. That smell is <the worst>. I used to wait until I was a few shops away and then run past holding my nose and covering my mouth.

I still can't believe some of the things I've eaten in the name of YouTube. I obviously go doolally sometimes and I always tell myself, 'Come on Saff, you're doing it for the viewers.'

It makes no sense that I'll eat all of those disgusting things but I won't really try anything that's outside my comfort zone at home. My mum tries to cook me new things and I'm like, 'NO', and I don't like certain combinations. I'll eat lasagne, but I won't eat spaghetti bolognaise, although my mum insists the only real difference between them is a cheese sauce and different shaped pasta.

I won't eat any kind of seafood and my worst foods ever are Brussels sprouts, cauliflower and mashed potato. Whenever I say that to people, they're horrified, because I think I'm the only person in the world who doesn't like mash. But it's . . . eurgh!

It's awful when I've gone round to new friends' houses and I've been served it for dinner. I feel so awkward. I used to eat it to be polite but I can't do it anymore, because as soon as I put it to my mouth I think I'm going to be sick. It's not the taste as much as the texture. It makes me gag. It's just so, like, mashy!

I've done a couple of pizza challenges on YouTube where I've had to race people to finish them, and I find that so upsetting because it's such a waste, when I love it. I don't even get to actually taste it because I have to eat so fast.

My absolute favourite thing to eat is a roast dinner. I'd have one every day if I could. But I never have sprouts or cauliflower with it. My mum hates going to carveries, but that's my idea of properly living it up. You could take my to the poshest restaurant in the world and I'd be like, 'It was okay.' But take to me a Toby Carvery, and I feel like I'm being shown a good time.

I love chicken and turkey, and I'll eat beef and lamb, but pork is a no-no. It's another thing that's on my list of foods I avoid. I could never be vegetarian. Can you imagine? Seeing as I basically live on chicken, I'd have nothing left to eat. I tasted some of that fake vegetarian chicken once and, I'm sorry, but it does not taste anything like it. It looks like someone has got luncheon meat and sapped the colour out of it. And it tastes like a dish sponge (not that I've actually eaten one, but I can totally imagine).

I'd love to like loads of foods, but it's just not happening. It's the same with tea and coffee. I really want to like one of them so I can go to tons of coffee shops and get those cups that are as big as your head. If I go to Starbucks with my friends, I'll have a hot chocolate or a smoothie, which I love, but it's not the same as ordering a really complicated coffee and thinking your life is complete when the baristas get it right.

HOT FOOD TIP! Peri-tamer sauce from Nando's is <amazing>. Not many people know about it because it's on the kids' menu but it's worth discovering. It's a sweet barbecue dressing with zero heat and it tastes so good. Also, if you ask for it after you've paid you get it for free. But don't tell Nando's I told you.

I can't enjoy Nando's as much if I don't have it, and the people I've told about it feel like they owe me a lifelong debt (please don't feel like you do, but do feel free to send food-related gifts by way of a thank you).

I also met up with an agent called Biff (IKR? Such a weird name), and he said he would be able to make me loads of money in a really short amount of time by expanding my brand and 'hammering it to death'.

The money sounds like a dream scenario, but when I spoke

to Mum about it, she said I needed to be thinking about my career as a long-term thing and not just a quick fix. It's a fair point. What if I work really hard for a year, make my millions and then it all goes quiet? I know it sounds mad, but I would much rather earn less money and have a longer career. Although, I also want enough money to be able to go shopping in all the designer stores on Rodeo Drive and not have to look at price tags. I can't imagine what that feels like. I'm still that girl who pretends I'm looking at the size on the label in high street stores when really I'm looking at how much it costs and thinking, 'How many tops like this would I be able to get in Primark for the same money?'

I don't think I'll ever be overly flashy and only wear things if they're designer. I always think if you've got some nice sunglasses and a bag, they somehow make everything else look more expensive. I don't go anywhere without my Louis Vuitton backpack and, even if I'm wearing a dress that cost £5, the bag brings the outfit up. In my opinion! It's all about how you wear things. As long as you wear something with confidence you can get anywhere.

Half the time I prefer high street clothes, and then you don't feel guilty when you go off them after only wearing them once. Which, I must admit, I'm pretty guilty of. My mum is always telling me off when she finds things I've been totally in love with the day I've bought them, and then I've worn them once and put them in a drawer and forgotten about them. And then probably gone and bought another thing just the same.

But I won't have that problem out here. Leonie said I can borrow her clothes anytime, so now I have two wardrobes to choose from!

I absolutely love shopping, but I can't go to the shops in January. They're such a mess and it's really weird because it's like stores go to their warehouses and scoop up everything that hasn't sold over the past two years. You'll find bikinis and summer dresses in among thick winter coats and fleecy socks. It makes no sense! I can't be bothered to spend ages looking through everything just in case I find something I love.

I also get hanger anger, when everything is attached to each other because there are too many clothes on the rail. If you try to pull one hanger out, you get about five different things. One of them is always woollen, so then the hangers get caught up on it and it's <so> irritating.

I tend to spend all my Christmas money on clothes, and I do impulse buy online. I'm bad for getting really excited and buying something because it's really cheap, and then when I look at it again it's somehow morphed into something hideous. My nan always says you should ask yourself if you'd pay full price for something you'd buy in a sale. If the answer is no, don't buy it, because you obviously don't like it that much. I get a bit carried away and think, 'Well, I might wear it.' Who ever really stops and thinks about whether they'll wear something if it's, like, two quid?

February 7th

I've signed with Steve and the company he works for, Magical Rainbows Media!!! I had some head shots done today, so he can send them out to casting agents, and it was so much fun. I love getting my hair and make-up done professionally, and the make-up artist did the most amazing eye wing I've ever seen. It was perfection. I've got pretty good with mine but this was Ariana Grande level, which is the dream.

My hair was also curled so well, I wish I could wake up with it like that every morning. It was so pretty, and everyone on the shoot was so kind to me.

The photographer was such a strange man. He was a proper surfer guy and he kept saying things to me like, 'Tell the camera you're a winner' and 'Give me those "I mean

business eyes", Saffron'. I kept trying not to laugh. Did he want my eyes to start wearing a power suit and carrying a briefcase?

I first started wearing make-up when I was in Year Eight. But it wasn't like a full face or anything, I think I was a bit young for all that. I'd wear a tiny bit of blusher and I built it from there. The next thing I introduced was eyeliner. Only not very well.

When I look back at my high-school pictures I cringe so hard. When I began wearing liquid eyeliner at the end of Year Eight, I could not do it <at all>. It was so thick. I used to try my best to do the Ariana wing and it did not work. One side would always be longer than the other and, because I used a cheap liner, the minute I touched my eyes, it would smear everywhere.

My friends were obviously trying to subtly tell me that it didn't look good, because they'd say things like, 'You look so much nicer without liner!' But I was a bit obsessed. It's painful to see how embarrassingly bad it was. I've had to take all the pictures off Facebook, so no one can see them.

I can do a really good wing now, but it's one of those things you have to practise. I always used to think I'd never be able to master eyeliner, but I hate being defeated, so one week I made a pact with myself that I'd practise every day until I got it. Some people use the tape technique, where you stick tape to the edge of your eye and draw over it, but I feel really smug about the fact that I don't need to do that now, because I worked so hard on it.

I got the hang of it after watching YouTube tutorials, and eventually I cracked it. It was quite a moment, and I couldn't wait to tell all my mates.

The best eyeliner I've found is the Kat Von D liner, which is like a felt-tip pen and it's so easy to use. Honestly, anyone can do a good flick with that if they try. Once it's in place, it doesn't shift or smudge, and discovering it has ever so slightly changed my life.

Steve's company is setting up some proper acting auditions for me, so Leonie and I spent today practising some lines from famous films just for fun, and also for when I have to go and meet people. Apparently, the auditions themselves can be pretty intimidating, because there will be loads of other people there and you have to act in front of a panel of people.

They also film it and, if they don't think you're very good, they can be really mean and they'll actually tell you. I do not like the sound of that at all, but if I want to go into acting I'm going to have to be pretty resilient.

It's mad in LA, because literally every other person you meet wants to be famous. Every waitress and valet and bellboy is here because they want to make it. It's funny, because on the one hand it feels like everyone is in the same boat and we've got this bond. But on the other hand, every person you meet is competing against you. You don't get that in Brighton!

February 13th

There's still no word on any auditions because Steve is waiting for the right thing to come in, but so much other stuff has been happening.

I know it's been a while since I mentioned Ryan, but that's because he's been away on a modelling job in Australia for, like, two weeks. We've been texting each other non-stop and he's coming back soon, which I'm super excited about. I still can't believe I've met someone so amazing, especially after my last disastrous relationship.

I also met Beth and she is the <best>. She came round to Leonie's and we had a girls' night in, where we did the usual thing of putting on face packs and watching movies. We also got takeout and the choice out here is ridiculous. You can get all the usual stuff, like pizza and burgers, but you can also order in salads and juices. Everyone is so health-conscious, and yet you can buy junk food everywhere you turn. It makes me wonder who's eating it all!

I miss my friends back home, and it's hard not having them around to go shopping with or hang out with. I usually see or speak to them every day, especially all my BFFs, and my friend Grace is always texting to find out how I'm getting on.

It's great that I'm meeting such nice people over here, and I know I'll make more friends the more time I spend here, but I guess it's different when you haven't known someone that long.

I've mainly been spending my days filming and editing videos. It's more important than ever that I keep everyone back home updated with what I'm doing. I don't want my viewers to forget about me!

February 14th

Happy Valentine's Day, everyone! Well, it's happy for everyone who's in a relationship, but it's basically rubbish for anyone who isn't. Ryan is still away – not that I'm suggesting we would have done anything together anyway – so Leonie, Beth and I are going out for dinner tonight to celebrate being fabulous, (sort of) single ladies. I'm dreaming of Nando's, but they haven't been kind enough to open one in LA especially for me yet, so we're going to another place that Leonie swears will be just as good. I'm very sceptical but we'll see. How can anything be as good as Nando's?

V Day is great if you've got a boyfriend, but so depressing if you don't. This year, 2017, was the first one for a while that I was single so I bought myself some presents instead.

If no one else is going to buy you nice things, there's nothing wrong with self-gifting.

I did get a bouquet of flowers from a mystery admirer and that was really nice, but it's really annoying me that I still don't know who they're from. Mum swears they're not from her, so I keep asking her about them in case she cracks.

Valentine's Day is just another day if you're single and it's quite annoying when you see people showing off their presents and cards and 'surprise' dinners all over the internet. I can't complain, though, because I was that kid who put it everywhere when I was with my ex, so I must have been really irritating. Sorry everyone!

My mum is so sweet, because she bought me and my brothers cards and presents and heart-shaped lollipops the whole time we were growing up. She'd always sign them with two hearts and never put her name on them, but we totally knew they were from her. It meant if anyone at school asked if I got a card, I could tell them I did!

I went on a school skiing trip on Valentine's Day one year and when I opened my suitcase, my mum had packed a card and a box of chocolates for me, so I didn't feel totally left out. I actually nearly cried. Mum only stopped doing it last year, because Jed said he was over it, but I'd be happy for her to carry on doing it. I'm always open to presents of any kind.

February is quite miserable, but it does give me some hope

that spring is on the way. And Mini Eggs make a comeback in the shops ready for Easter, and that makes me so happy. It makes no sense that they don't sell them all year round. <Why, Cadbury, why?>

* * *

February 15th

Guys, it turns out I was right. The restaurant was really cute and it was decked out like a '50s diner with high stools and American road signs. The food was good but it was <not> Nando's standard. I had chicken and corn on the cob, and they put some kind of weird salsa stuff on the side that I had to try, and I felt like my mouth was going to explode. Leonie and Beth said it didn't have any heat to it, but they must have Teflon mouths because it was <scorching>.

After dinner, we went for a walk because I wanted to check out the local area. It's a pretty unusual thing to do in LA. No one walks anywhere. They drive around in massive cars and there's valet parking everywhere, which costs a fortune. I think it would be pretty hard to be poor and live in LA.

February 20th

Ryan is back! He came to see me earlier and he bought me a present from Australia. It was a snow globe with the Sydney Opera House inside that I strongly suspect he picked up at the airport on his way home, but it was still a nice thought. And to be honest, he could have bought me a bag of chillies and I would still have been happy (and I really, really, really hate chillies).

We went to the cinema this afternoon and we had such a good day. He's got a better tan than ever and he was wearing these black skinny jeans and a plain white T-shirt, which is one of my favourite looks.

I'm not kidding, I've always had an idea of what my ideal man would be like, and this is it:

My Perfect Man

1) *He'd have Zac Efron's face and his dark-brown hair and blue eyes. Oh, and his eyebrows. So his face, generally.*
2) *He'd have Grayson or Ethan Dolan or Nate Garner's really sharp jawline.*
3) *He'd have Zac Efron's body. I realize this guy is quite Zac-heavy.*

4) *He'd have Brooklyn Beckham's style.*
5) *He'd have Kevin Hart's personality, because he's really funny.*

Those five things basically describe Ryan. It's like I made him up. Maybe I'm some kind of witch who can conjure up exactly what she wants without realizing it? I'm going to ask for a million pounds and a never-ending supply of chocolate raisins next.

February 23rd

I've got my first audition on March 3rd! Steve asked me if I'd ever done any singing before so I told him about my band, Born2Blush. I know it's a terrible name. What can I say? We were young.

Apparently some big–name producer types are working on a new film about a band and they're looking for a female lead singer. I'm not counting my chickens but <imagine> if I got it?

I was in Born2Blush from the age of fourteen to fifteen, and it had always been a big dream of mine. I was in the band with three of my best friends, who I'd known for years. We all went to the same singing club and the guy who ran it had been talking about putting a band together for a while. One day he asked us if we fancied becoming a group, and we were all like, 'Yeeeeeeeees!'

We did four-part harmonies and we really looked up to bands like Destiny's Child and En Vogue, because their vocals are crazily on point. We so wanted to be like them.

We'd practise after school and at weekends, and we were getting somewhere and working on our own music. But then things started getting a bit tense within the band, and the busier things got, the more the cracks started to show.

We began going up to London a lot and the band took up more and more of our time, and some of the other girls weren't that happy about it. Sadly, that meant we started arguing because people were getting tired and not everyone was able to put in the same amount of effort.

Some of us had boyfriends and some didn't, so some of us had outside interests, while others wanted to focus solely on the band. We were working with a great record company, but they could see that there was some friction and, because of that, they decided it wasn't really working out and they didn't want to work with us any longer. That was a huge blow, because it felt like just as a door was opening for us, it was slammed in our faces again.

The record company even said to us, 'The problem is, you don't even seem like you're really friends.' But the stupid thing is, we were, and we had been for years, and we thought the world of each other. But we were letting pointless things get to us, and that was our downfall.

It was horrible that the band started to affect how we were with each other on a friendship level too. The more successful we got, the more pressure we were under, and the less fun it became.

We had an original song of our own, and before that we did a lot of covers and mash-ups that we'd put up on YouTube. We got really positive feedback, and off the back of that we were contacted to try out for *The X Factor.*

Usually, you have to go through four auditions before you even see the judges, but they wanted to fast-track us straight through. Some of us wanted to go for it and some didn't, so in the end it didn't happen, because we couldn't come to an agreement.

We did end up trying out for *Britain's Got Talent,* because we thought it would be good experience, but we didn't even plan to take it all the way and go on TV or anything. It was more of a test to see if our hearts were really in it and, sadly, we soon discovered that not everyone's was.

Another problem was that some girls were quite bitchy to us. Some of the haters were really mean, which was unfair because we were just trying to do something fun. We could all sing and we worked so hard.

Sometimes the other kids at school would play our songs on loudspeaker when we walked into the canteen, and then they'd all look at us and laugh. I'm lucky, in that I'm confident about what I do, so I'd brush off the comments or the jokes, but not all of the other girls in the band found it that easy, and it got to them.

I think some people had been jealous because we were so close and we did everything together. I always loved that about us, so it was even sadder when things started to crumble.

People do find it hard to get their heads around others doing something different. Half of the people who took the mickey out of us probably wanted to do the same thing themselves, but it was much easier to laugh at us than put in the work and do the same thing themselves.

As a band we had some real laughs, and I'm really glad I did it. I've always been happy as long as I'm performing, and we got to experience all kinds of things. We entered competitions and we performed at a few small events, and it was really cool while it lasted.

When the band broke up, I was pretty devastated and it was a really confusing time. We'd spent so much time together and then all of a sudden I was back to being on my own again. The band took up most of our spare time, and I was used to being busy every hour of every day, and there's only so much shopping someone can do!

I always thought my career would be about singing and I felt like I lost direction, so I had to try and find out what I wanted to do next. I've always hoped I'll get another opportunity to sing, and also do some more acting, so I'll have to see what the future brings.

February 28th

My family FaceTimed me this evening and they were all having pancakes for Shrove Tuesday. The Americans aren't big on Pancake Day (which is weird, because they're really big on pancakes). It made me feel really sad, because it's such a big tradition in our house and it felt so strange not to be there for it.

We always have a pancake-flipping competition at home and it's irritating because Casey is really good at it and always wins.

(Casey: 'Of course I do. I'm a genius.')

It also felt odd not being there for Mum and Jed's birthdays, because we always spend them together. We usually go out for dinner as a family and those are some of my favourite times. It also means I get to buy presents. I like giving presents almost as much as I like giving them.

I love buying presents because I love seeing people's reactions. I'll buy stuff <way> in advance because I get so excited. My mum is super hard to buy for though, because she's so ridiculously honest. She would rather you saved your money than got her something she doesn't really want. You either have to get her something she loves or not get her anything at all. Jed's pretty easy. I can give him money and he'll be happy. Who doesn't like money?

My guide to buying presents:

* Think about what your friend likes, not what you like.

* Look through your friend's Instagram for inspiration.
* Don't be too literal. Just because your friend likes apples, don't buy her a bag of apples.
* If you really love what you buy them, make sure you buy one for yourself.

CHAPTER 3

MARCH

MARCH 2ND

February was such a good month so I don't know how March is going to top it. But then, tomorrow is my big audition so if I land that role then no month, ever, will top this one. I've been rehearsing loads and Steve has told me to go in there with a smile on my face and act like the part was already mine. I'm worried that might come off as a bit arrogant so I'll play things down slightly. I don't want the casting directors to think I'm really overconfident.

March 3rd

O. M. G. Yesterday was honestly one of the most terrifying days of my life. I was expecting there to be a lot of people auditioning but this was <ridiculous>. And the weird thing was, most of the girls looked pretty much the same.

I got given some lines to read over and, as I was sat in the waiting room, I was looking around thinking, 'This is a room full of MEs!' It was like being in a room at Madame Tussauds that had been filled with Saffron Barker-alikes.

I was so nervous before I went in to see the casting directors. Leonie gave me a lift there, so at least I was on time (I cannot get my head around the buses in LA – I swear they all to go different places than it says on the front of them), and I kept telling myself I could do it.

I'd chosen my outfit really carefully. I wanted something that was cute but didn't scream, 'Look, I've dressed up to impress you!' Steve said they would want to see someone who was like the character, which was a 17-year-old girl who moves to LA to make it big (sound familiar?). After discussing it with Leonie at length, I wore some dark-blue skinny jeans, a candy-pink ripped, distressed top and some new white Vans.

I got called in and I had to stand in front of a panel of

five people, state my name and my experience (does playing Annie count?) and then read my lines.

The reality of what I was going through hit me, and I heard my voice wobble slightly at one point. But I took a deep breath and carried on as if nothing had happened. If in doubt, blag it.

The room was deathly silent and I started panicking that my phone was going to ring, even though I'd switched it to airplane mode, and then switched it off completely.

No one on the panel said a single word, and their blank expressions gave nothing away. When I finished my audition, one woman said, 'Thanks, we'll let you know!' and that was it. My time was up. I was in there for less than five minutes. Was that a good sign? A bad sign? Was it a sign of anything?

I had to phone Mum as soon as I left, because I really needed to hear her voice. The whole thing was just so . . . weird. I guess it was because it was so new, but it made me feel kind of anxious.

I know people think I'm super confident. And really, I am, but we all have our moments, and that was definitely one of them. I guess because so much was at stake, I put a lot of pressure on myself.

Mum was really supportive and said to me:

'Saffron, we all have challenges and things we have to face. If you want something, it doesn't always just drop into your

lap. You probably did a lot better than you thought and, if you don't get this role, there will be another one that will be even better for you. You're a hard worker and you deserve success, but that doesn't always mean it's guaranteed. And don't ever worry about having a wobble. Even superstars do. Look at all the celebrities, from Lady Gaga to Justin Bieber, who admit they feel insecure sometimes. You wouldn't be human if you didn't worry.'

That was just the kick up the backside I needed. Mum was right. This was my first-ever professional audition. And it was in Hollywood, of all places! That was achievement enough. Sometimes it's so much easier to give yourself a hard time than a pat on the back (have you ever actually tried to give yourself a pat on the back? Unless you've got unnaturally long arms, it's really tough).

In my opinion, we're never really kind enough to ourselves, and this was one of those times where I had to give myself a break. So what if I didn't walk in and smash it? Who cares if they didn't all faint at the sight of my brilliance, and actually barely looked at me instead? It didn't mean I was any less great. It said a lot more about them than it did about me.

I hope it doesn't sound like I think I'm, like, totally amazing or anything, but I would say I'm a pretty self-assured person and I would probably give myself an eight out of ten for confidence. I realize that's pretty high, and I'm very lucky to feel like that, but I do work at it too.

I always build myself up and tell myself I'm capable of doing things. I don't just hope for the best. I make sure I work hard and I achieve the things I want to, and that keeps me feeling good.

There have been loads of times when I've had to fake it to make it. When I was in the girl band, I used to get so nervous about performing in front of crowds, and the other girls and I were always boosting each other up before a competition or gig.There have been times when I've been at events and my mum's had to pretty much push me onto a stage because I'm terrified.

Once I've done the speech or whatever, and I've got past that initial fear, I know I can do it again. It's all about doing it for the first time, and then knowing you'll be able to do it for the second and third time and so on. Sometimes you only get good at things by actually doing them.

My mum always says, 'What's the worst thing that's going to happen if something doesn't go well? Is the world going to end?' And she's right. Anytime things have gone a bit wrong in the past, people have been really sweet and supportive rather than laughing at me. It's not like people are out to get you and they want to watch a stage fail. They're there to see you, so why would they want that?

I'll never forget this one time, I was invited along to this show to meet viewers. It was an event that was put on by a beauty brand and I was having one of 'those' days. My skin had broken out a bit, nothing I tried on felt right and I wanted to crawl back into my bed and wrap the duvet really tightly around me.

As always, it was Mum who said to me, 'Saff, just because you don't feel great, doesn't mean you don't look great. No one will think you look any different to how you usually do except you. Slap on a smile and make the most of it, and I bet you an hour after you arrive you'll be having so much fun you'll have forgotten about your morning meltdown.' And guess what? She wasn't wrong.

I always think the best films are the ones where people have some kind of incredible triumph after something really bad happens. Always remember that, even if things get bad, you can come back stronger. If you get knocked down, get back up again and smile even harder.

Sometimes I'll look at photos of myself with fans and think, 'They have no idea I didn't feel good about myself that day, because I look so happy.' And, honestly, that's all they will have seen. Me, smiling. They won't have noticed the annoying curl that was facing the wrong way that I was fixating on, or the MASSIVE spot that was brewing on my chin (that was probably embarrassingly small). All they'll have been thinking is, 'Yay! I met Saffron, and she was really nice to me!' How cool is that?

I love meeting my viewers, and they really do mean so much to me. I get recognized in the most random places. One of the weirdest was probably in a public toilet in Las Vegas, when I was washing my hands. This really sweet girl came over and asked if she could give me a hug and I was like, 'Erm, you might want to wait for me to dry my hands first!' It turned out she didn't, and she gave me a hug anyway!

I get stopped a lot when I go shopping, and quite often girls will see on my Twitter or Instagram feed that I'm in a certain town, so they'll head to the same place to see if they can spot me. It's incredible how many people do find me. They know me so well, they know exactly which shops I'll be going to. They check them all out just in case, and they usually find me paying for something in one of them!

I have never, ever had a bad fan experience, but I have had a really funny one. I was in Debenhams in Brighton, buying make-up with another friend of mine who's a YouTuber. I was getting stopped by a lot of people and asked for pictures because people around the area know me, but she's not from Brighton, so not as many people recognized her.

This young girl was with her mum and she was super excited when she spotted us, she was almost in tears. She was too nervous to come over, but her mum walked up to me and said, 'My daughter said you're a YouTuber and she watches you every single day. Can she get a picture with you?'

This little girl was freaking out, so I went to hug her and she said to her mum really loudly, 'No, she's not the one I'm talking about. It's the other one!' CRINGE!

The girl's mum said, 'Oh, sorry, I didn't realize you weren't a YouTuber. My mistake. Can she have a photo with your friend?'

How embarrassing? It was so awkward. I ended up having to take the photo too, which was even worse. Such a fail.

I think it's so sweet, but I always feel terrible when people start crying when they meet me because I want to make sure they're okay. I went to the Arndale Centre in Manchester and I got a bit mobbed, and a security guard came over and told me I had to leave the mall because there was such a crowd. I've had to be escorted around before, and I feel so ridiculous! Like I think I'm Beyoncé or something!

My parents have given me a lot of advice as I've grown up and, like most kids, I've have no choice but to listen to it. It's so frustrating when you don't want to believe something they say ('You'll feel better tomorrow' is one of the worst sayings), because it goes against everything you're feeling. But you know deep down they only want the best for you and they're only trying to help.

My mum and dad are both very caring but also very matter-of-fact about things, and sometimes what you need most is someone you love to be totally honest with you. The thing about family is that you can say pretty much anything to each other and know that, no matter how angry you feel, you'll have to forgive them at some point!

My mum is always supportive of me, but that doesn't mean she always agrees with me. If she thinks I'm in the wrong, if I argue with Jed or Casey and she thinks it's my fault, she'll tell me. Or if she thinks I shouldn't do something, she won't hold back. I don't always appreciate it at the time, but I guess I always do later on!

It's hard to admit you're not always right, but I've had to come to terms with the fact that not even <I'm> perfect! I'm not much of a sulker, so even if Mum and I do have a fallout, it's usually fine pretty quickly.

The worst argument we had was when we had to get to a meeting in London and I wanted to pay for a top I fell in love with in a clothes shop. The queue was massively long, but I was worried that if I didn't get it there and then, it would sell out and I'd be gutted.

In the end, Mum made me put it back on the rail and we rushed to the meeting. When we went back to the shop to get the top afterwards, there were none left in my size and I was so irrationally cross with Mum that I didn't speak to her for the entire journey home.

It was only when I'd calmed down that Mum pointed out that if we'd been late to that meeting, I could have missed out on a big work opportunity. And – sigh – once again, she was right. And, anyway, I managed to buy the top online so everything worked out in the end 😂.

Mum gives me tough love when it's necessary, but she's also the kindest person I know. After I split up with my ex, I was so upset and she was really worried about me, so she slept in my bed with me night after night, cuddling me while I cried.

Of all the advice Mum's given me, there's one thing that's stuck with me more than anything. Are you ready for this bit of life-changing wisdom?

'Always go in the first cubicle in a public toilet because it's the one that always used the least.'

Now I know that you'll wonder how you got this far in life without that advice in your brain.

My three top tips for believing in yourself

* Remember no one's perfect. <No>one.
* Know that it's not how hard you fall, but how gracefully you get up that matters.
* You are GREAT. I said so. And if I said it, it must be true.

March 11th

So, I heard back about the audition and I didn't get the part. But instead of letting it get me down, I'm going to use it to drive myself forward and focus on the next thing. One audition doesn't mean I've failed. The fact that I even turned up when I was so nervous is a massive win.

I'm having a catch-up with Steve today to talk about how we're going to expand the Saffron Barker brand into America. Woop! He wants me to start doing much more regular vlogs and apparently US companies have already been in touch about wanting to do stuff with me. And – I-literally-can't-believe-this-is-happening alert – this really cool American clothing brand have asked if I want to fly to New York to do a trip and vlog about it. Er, YES.

March 15th

Remember that trip I told you about? I'm on it! And the best thing is, they said I could bring someone with me and they agreed to fly Mum out from the UK. I'm still in a bit of shock.

As much as being in LA is amazing, it's weird not being able to do little things. I love my crazy fam and I miss them more each day (even Casey), so I can't wait to see Mum. I'll be arriving before her so she's going to meet me at the hotel tomorrow and we're going to go exploring.

Did I mention that the hotel is like something you'd see on a TV show about the richest people in the world? You know, one of those shows you pretend you don't like watching but, as soon as you catch a glimpse, it's like your eyeballs have been glued to the TV screen? Yeah, <that>.

Mum and I are sharing a room, and I was expecting us to have to snuggle up in a little double bed. Uh-uh. We have a suite, everyone. It's massive, with two king-size beds, a living room and a bathroom, with the biggest bath in it you've ever seen. You could fit an entire boy band in it and still have room for their entourage.

I swear, you could fit my bedroom at home into the suite, like, fifteen times. It's so cool. We are so going to make the most of it. I don't have to be at the event until the day after tomorrow, so I've booked Mum and me for massages in the spa, followed by afternoon tea. That always sounds really posh, but it basically means we get to eat loads of cakes, doesn't it?

March 17th

Mum is here and it's the best thing ever! We had such a cool day yesterday, and as soon as I saw her I felt my shoulders drop. I hadn't even realized I'd been stressed, but the moment she hugged me I relaxed and I felt like 17-year-old Saffron from Brighton again.

We're off to the fashion event today, which involves us watching a fashion show and then chatting to some viewers afterwards. I love going to these kinds of events because, at the end of the day, I'm only a YouTuber because people take the time to watch my videos.

In the taxi to the fashion show, Mum broke the earth-shattering news that Dad has signed up to run a marathon. Like, what? WHAT? This cannot be true. My dad is lazy! I emailed him straight away to get to the bottom of it (I don't generally email much, but Dad is old school).

To: Darrenbarker@thisisweird.com
From: SaffronBarker@themoon.com
Subject: I'm so confused

Dad, it's come to my attention that you're running a marathon. How can this be true? Please explain.

....

To: SaffronBarker@themoon.com
From: Darrenbarker@thisisweird.com
Subject: Re: I'm so confused

Dear Daughter, your information is correct, and of course I'll explain. A marathon is a long run that people do to raise money for charity. I hope that clears things up for you.

....

To: Darrenbarker@thisisweird.com
From: SaffronBarker@themoon.com
Subject: Re: I'm so confused

Haha, Dad. Very funny, you know what I mean. What's happened to you since I left? I don't understand. If someone asked me to give a list of the people in the universe I thought would never run a marathon, you'd be at the top of it.

Why, why, why?

....

To: SaffronBarker@themoon.com
From: Darrenbarker@thisisweird.com
Subject: Re: I'm so confused

Your mum made me do it.

....

To: Darrenbarker@thisisweird.com
From: SaffronBarker@themoon.com
Subject: Re: I'm so confused

Okay. It all makes sense now. Love you x

....

March 18th

Yesterday was just the best fun. There were loads of other YouTubers at the fashion show, and this guy called TuBot told me he was coming to LA next week and wants to make a video with me. This is <massive>. He's one of the biggest YouTubers in America. He's got almost ten million subscribers, and he literally wants us to work together 😀😀😀😀😀😀😀😀😀😀😀😀😀😀😀😀😀😀😀😀.

YouTube has been a massive life-changer for me. I've been creating videos for about two years, and I first started vlogging my life when I was in Florida. It was after that that I set up my channel, and I've never looked back.

I'd always watched YouTubers like Zoella, Marcus and Alfie and thought they were so cool, but I was too nervous to do my own. I'd been with my boyfriend for six months at that point and I'd already appeared in some of his vlogs. People kept saying, 'Saffron needs to make her own channel.' I guess that kind of encouraged me.

It also coincided with the band splitting up. I'd been so busy rehearsing and performing with them, and now I had all this spare time on my hands. I'm not one of those people who likes spending days doing nothing, and I needed a new project.

Even though I was already kind of known by some people on YouTube via my ex, I was nervous about launching myself and maybe being judged. It was more to do with what people would say about me than anything else. As anyone who's read the comments on YouTube knows, people can be pretty harsh at times.

I was used to being judged for being in the band by other people at school, and that was hard enough. I thought launching my own channel would probably end up being an extension of that and no one likes to read horrible things about themselves, no matter how confident or resilient they are.

I think you've got to be pretty strong as a YouTuber. I found it hard at first, because no one thought that I was ever going to make it. They also assumed I thought I was really great because I was putting myself out there, but that <so> wasn't the case. In fact, rather than it being a massive confidence-booster, it was actually quite a self-esteem drain at times, because of the things people said.

You have to force yourself not to worry about what others think. I know a lot of people would have stopped straight away if they'd come up against negativity. You have to block out the noise that you get from people who don't love what you're doing. Or who do love what you're doing, but don't want to admit it!

I was lucky because I had loads of support from my family when I first started out, and they always encouraged me. As soon as I said I wanted to do YouTube, they all kind of rushed to my side and they were there when I needed them. Even Jed, although he did find it difficult.

As we all know, Jed's not a big fan of the camera and he found it quite embarrassing. Sometimes he'd come home and say, 'So-and-so said this about Saffron today.' He'd be quite upset because it was almost like it was happening to him too.

The more well-known I got, the more Jed hated it, because the people who didn't know me didn't like how well I was doing. My real friends were pleased for me, but the people who only knew of me used it as an excuse to take the mickey as much as possible.

Jed would stick up for me and then he'd end up getting hassle, which was the last thing he needed. I felt bad that he was kind of dragged into it, but the only way to stop that would have been to give up totally, and I would always have regretted it.

There was never a point when I thought, 'This is too hard.' There were some videos that got a lot of hate, and I'd always debate whether or not I should take them down. I never did, though, because I thought I'd be the one to miss out if I did.

Sometimes I'd get upset about hate, and there were days when it chipped away at me and I had to rise above it. YouTube was what I wanted to do and I couldn't pander to other people's jealousy or I'd miss out. And the chances were, if I stopped doing it, one of the people who had been slagging me off would probably try and jump into my place, and how annoying would that be?!

Did I ever think about putting it on hold or waiting until I left school? Nah. I'd dread Monday mornings because I always put videos up on a Sunday evening, so that's when things would kick off, but I always knew Tuesday would be better. Then Wednesday would be easier still, and then Thursday . . . You get the picture! And it was never unmanageable.

I've always felt really lucky to be doing what I do. I knew

I just had to get through the tricky bits and then it would be okay again. It's like when you spend hours in the hairdresser, bored of out of your mind. You know your hair's going to look amazing at the end of it, so you sit it out and it's all worth it in the end.

I remember filming a 'What's in my bag?' video, and the following day at school people would be saying to each other, 'What's in your bag today?' in front of me to take the mickey. It wasn't nasty, it was just stupid.

The silly thing was that I used to read all the comments, and there could be a million nice ones, but I'd find one horrible one and that would be it. It's always that one that sticks in your mind. I used to Google people's names to try and find out who they were and why they had such an issue with me. So many of them were from Brighton, which I found sad. You would have thought they'd be the ones that were supportive when they were from my home town.

The boys were way worse than the girls in a way. The girls would say stuff on the internet, whereas boys would say things to my face. Because I'm a really honest person, I did prefer that, because I would rather they had the front to be real. But when you've got someone standing in front of you, telling you you're crap, it isn't nice.

Now it doesn't bother me as much. I do still get trolled sometimes but I've toughened up. Weirdly, I seem to get more negative comments the happier I am, which makes no sense. My favourite vlogs ever have the most hate. People pick on the most pathetic things ever. How can they even be bothered?

I was so nervous about putting up my first official video, I literally waited until I was out of the country because I thought it would be safer. Even if people did say nasty things, I was thousands of miles away, so hopefully it wouldn't sting as much.

I was in Florida for three weeks during my summer holidays, and I bought some equipment at the airport with my birthday money so I'd be ready to get started when I got out there. I bought a big DSLR camera, but I found it quite fiddly, so I started off doing videos on my phone using a selfie stick (back when they were really popular!).

These days I can film a video in one take and then edit it, but my first one was a disaster. I did the same take at least twenty times. I was walking back and forth through the door of Busch Gardens saying, 'I'm at Busch Gardens!' really excitedly. I must have looked like such an idiot. I was doing it again and again and again. People were staring at me and I felt so self-conscious. I didn't feel like any of the takes for my videos were good enough and they didn't look <at all> natural. So in the end, I chose the one that was the <least> bad. That's not exactly a goal, is it?

I was so nervous, and you could tell because it looked unnatural. I wasn't used to walking around talking into my phone like it was a person. There wasn't a single time when I relaxed and let it flow because, in my head, I was going, 'What's that girl over there going to think about what I'm saying?'

These days, I don't care who sees me. I just whip out my camera and off I go. It's weirder if I'm on my own, because people probably think I've got an imaginary friend. The more videos I've made, the less I care how stupid I look!

I tried to be more natural in my next video, so I casually walked through the door of our hotel and said, 'Morning!' in a really cheery voice. I ended up doing it about thirty times, so by the time I finished, I didn't feel very cheery. I can't watch that video back now because it's so awful. I was so drained by the end of it.

My concentration wasn't great, either, so I used to walk into doors and trip over things. Also, my selfie stick had a wire that linked the stick and my phone but mine broke, so I was always dropping my phone mid-take. Usually when I was halfway through actually doing a good video, which is typical.

Another thing I'd do is film what I thought was a really cool video. I'd go and tell my mum with a big smile on my face and she'd say, 'You do know you've got lipstick all over your teeth, right?' FAIL. Most of the time, I ended up using the videos anyway because I was so sick of trying to make them 'perfect'. It's funny, because I think the fact my videos are so natural is what people like most about them, but back then I was determined to make them look slick and professional.

All in all, I didn't get off to a great start.

Also, I'm pretty sure the trip to Florida was the start of Jed's phobia about being in my videos. He'd get so, so frustrated because we'd visit somewhere so I could film a video, and he knew it would take <forever>. He wanted to enjoy his holiday and have fun, and I'd be like, 'Can I just reshoot that bit? It was terrible! I'll only be another five minutes. Maybe ten. Make that an hour.'

When I look back at my first videos, I cringe so hard. That person just wasn't me. Well, obviously it was me, because if it wasn't me, it would be someone different. But you know what I mean? I had to do so many takes and you can really tell I wasn't very comfortable. My hand was even shaking while I was holding the camera. That's how nervous I was.

I would never take that video down because I think it's kind of sweet that I was so worried about it all. I wouldn't change it, because it shows how far I've come and how much better I've become through hard work. My mum reckons it's cute, but Jed reckons it's rubbish. Surprise!

I think the problem with my early videos is that I was trying to be someone else. I didn't have any originality. I'd watch Zoella and think I had to be like her. If I were to give anyone a piece of advice, it would be to be yourself because there's already a Zoella and a Naomi Smart, but there's not a 'you' out there yet.

If you're not being honest about who you are, it totally shows through. The most important thing with vlogging – and probably in life – is to be yourself. If you're not, you'll always get found out.It was great to watch other YouTubers to find out how they nailed being good at videos but, honestly, it was only when I started being myself that things fell into place and I started being more successful.

I was trying to be sensible and make videos that were flawless. But let's face it: this is me, so that was never going to happen. They're so much better now I don't overthink them, and I love how all over the place some of the recordings are. Some of my favourite moments are when someone walks into shot at a really important moment or something. That's what makes them unique.

I was so worried about what people I knew would think about the first video I uploaded, but the funny thing is that no one actually saw it. I had a semi-big Instagram follow from being in the band and appearing in my ex's videos, and most of those people were positive and nice. But I was waiting for comments from the kids I went to school with, and I was not looking forward to it.

I'd prepared myself for the worst, but I shouldn't have bothered because not one person mentioned it online or messaged me about it. No one. There wasn't any hate, there was just . . . nothing. My friend Georgie, who is one of my closest friends and always has my back throughout everything, was the only person who said well done to me, and that meant a lot. Everyone else? 🤐

Because no one discovered my first video, I got away without nasty comments for a while. But it was a different story when I put my second video up. Some of the boys in my year started doing Snapchats taking the mickey, and being pretty harsh.

Even boys I was mates with were laughing at the videos and putting them on their stories and being like <'What is she doing?'> It hurt more when it was people I considered to be friends. I texted one guy who I'd always got on really well with and asked him why he was taking the mickey out of me and he replied, 'Don't take it personally, it's just a laugh.' But when someone's mocking something that involves you, how can you not take it personally?

I was so nervous about going back to school after the holidays in case people were nasty, but it wasn't too bad. I got a few comments here and there, but it was bearable. Equally, no one said well done, either. I would totally have congratulated one of my friends if they'd been brave enough to put up some videos, but people seemed to have a weird issue with it.

A couple of people said I was trying to be like other YouTubers and, as much as I hate to admit it, at the time I probably was because I still hadn't found out who I was in that world.

I've always been the kind of person who knows what they want to do, and when I put my mind to something I'm pretty determined. If I focus on something I go for it. I know I won't get to where I want to be unless I do. At the end of the day, if I stop doing something because other people are telling me to, I'm the loser. I'm the one stopping myself from getting to where I want to then. That's what they want, not what I want, and it's not about them!

When people I knew in school went behind my back and said stuff about me, that was so painful. They'd be really friendly when they saw me, and then slag me off as soon as I wasn't around and I hate that. The one thing I can't stand is two-faced people. If you don't like me? That's fine and that's your choice, but I would rather you were upfront about things. I'm the total opposite. If I don't like someone, I'll tell them. Or I'll just be polite. But I would never suck up to someone and then go and slag them off on social media.

When I've been let down by people in the past, I've done my best to put it into perspective. The people I love in my life are the important ones and if someone is going to hate on me, it's their energy they're wasting. They're not having mine as well. I've got things I want to work towards, and

I've always been very clear about that. I can either let these people pull me back, or I can use them as giant rubber bands to ping me forward.

At the end of the day, the biggest revenge is success. That feeling of proving people wrong is the best thing ever. So every single one of the haters is helping you in a way. They're helping you to be more resilient, they're helping you to fight for what you want and they're helping you to realize how you don't want to be as a person. Because you sure as hell don't want to be where they are (I feel like I should waggle my index finger around or do what 'whatever' sign at this point)

Remember, use hate to motivate!

My favourite haters quotes

HATERS =
Having
Anger
Towards
Everyone
Reaching
Success

If you don't like me, and you still watch everything I do? B**ch, you're a fan!

The only person I'm in competition with is who I was yesterday.

March 18th continued . . .

Mum flies home tomorrow, and it's going to be so hard saying goodbye to her. A part of me wants to hop on the flight home with her, but I've made a commitment to stay in LA for a year and that's what I'll do. I am NOT the kind of person who gives up easily.

March 19th

Oh my god, I can't stop crying! I miss Mum so much! We were both in floods of tears when we left each other at the airport, and I don't know how I managed not to run all the way to her departure gate and follow her onto the plane (obviously there's also the small matter of me probably getting arrested).

LA is so amazing, but I miss my family, I do. I hate to admit it, but even though I've got Leonie and Beth and Ryan, somehow it doesn't feel the same as popping into the Churchill Centre and spending far too much in Superdrug before running up the escalator to the food court. I know it's not glamorous, but I would love to be able to zoom home and do that again right now.

Okay, moaning over. I'm going to dry my eyes and go and meet Ryan for a smoothie. The sun is shining and I bought some new Ray-Ban sunglasses, which means I've got the perfect way to hide the fact I've been sobbing for the last hour.

(Later the same day . . .)

I'm feeling loads better now. Ryan was so sweet earlier and he said he'd miss me loads if I went back home. How cute? It helps so much having him here. Although he's developed this really weird habit of watching literally everyone come and go when we go out, and I feel like he's not <always> concentrating on what I'm saying.

I've also got my video with TuBot to look forward to. He's coming into town from New York next week and he's emailed me some ideas (enough with the emailing, people!).

From: TuBot@imanidiotbutyoudontrealiseyet.com
To: Saffronbarker@themoon.com
Subject: Our cool as f@@k video

Hi Saffron, I've come up with some really cool ideas for our videos, and I'd love your feedback as soon as possible so I can get the wheels in motion. Peace out. TuBot x

* We pretend to be a couple and mess about and pretend to go on a date.
* You spot me in the street and pretend not to know who I am and you chase me and ask me out.
* We bump into each other in a coffee shop and you flirt with me and I pretend I'm into you. But then I spot a model and I go and ask her out instead and you're gutted.

....

Is anyone else sensing a theme here? One that involves me looking like an idiot and TuBot looking like he's basically irresistible?

I mean, he's pretty cute and all that, but he's no Ryan. And I'd rather not end up looking like some desperate girl who's in love with a guy who's not interested, even if it is just for fun. More importantly, I've never set up any of my videos so it would be <weird> if I started now.

From: Saffronbarker@themoon.com
To: TuBot@imanidiotbutyoudontrealiseyet.com
Subject: Re: Our cool as f@@k video

Hi TuBot, thanks for the suggestions. I think it would be better if we just did a straightforward video with us messing about, if that's cool with you? You know, we can chat? Or we could do a food challenge, or explore LA together and vlog it? Let me know what you think x

....

Oh god, I put a kiss. Should I have put a kiss? He put a kiss though. What's the etiquette on kisses? Is he going to think I fancy him? Can kisses just be considered friendly when you don't really know someone very well? Should I have deleted it? Would he have thought I was rude?

FOR GOD'S SAKE, SAFFRON, IT'S JUST AN EMAIL KISS! IT'S NOT LIKE YOU GAVE HIM A REAL ONE!

From: TuBot@imanidiotbutyoudontrealiseyet.com
To: Saffronbarker@themoon.com
Subject: Re: Our cool as f@@k video

Sure thing babycakes. Let's keep it real x

....

Babycakes? WTF?

March 26th

MY LIFE IS OVER. I'M GOING TO BE A YOUTUBE JOKE. WHY DID I EVER AGREE TO DO A VIDEO WITH TUBOT? OR TOOLBOT, AS HE WILL NOW BE KNOWN?

I honestly don't know where to start telling you the story of the worst day of my life. How about at the beginning? That could work.

ToolBot and I arranged to meet on Venice Beach to film our video this morning, and the four hours that followed were some of the worst I've ever experienced. I mean, I've watched his videos, and I'll admit that he's quite outrageous in some of them (the one where he made his nipples bleed when he was waxing his chest is a highlight), but <nothing> could have prepared me for this. He was loud, he was rude and he told the psychic I saw earlier in the year that she looked like she smelt of wee. I wanted to die.

We went and got ice creams and sat on the beach to finish off the video. TuBot asked some random guy who was walking past if he'd mind filming us (he didn't seem to think about the fact this guy could run off with his camera), and the second the guy pointed the camera in our direction, TuBot went in for the kill. And when I say kill, I mean kiss. And not just a peck on the cheek but a full-on, revolting, tongue-waggling snog.

I was so shocked I dropped my ice cream on his leg while I was trying to fight him off. TuBot's response? He 'dropped' his ice cream down my top and then started laughing like someone had just told him the best joke anyone's ever told, EVER.

I jumped up and screamed. Then I cried and shouted to the random stranger to stop filming. He didn't. I tried to shake the ice cream out from under my top but it was stuck, and it was <freezing>.

'What the hell do you think you're doing? Why on earth did you kiss me? What were you thinking?' I shouted at a grinning TuBot.

'Chill babes, it's only what we agreed!' he said, flicking his hair back and rolling his eyes.

Let me ask you all a question. You've seen the emails, right? At what point did I agree to kiss TuBot and let him make me look like a total dork? Never? Spot on!

Just as I thought I couldn't get any angrier, TuBot turned to the 'stranger', shrugged and said, 'Come on, dude, she's clearly not up for a laugh. Let's go and get a burger. I've got everything I needed. More British subscribers here I come!'

Oh god. I've been well and truly had.

CHAPTER 4

April

April 1st

Well, I've done it. I've become the biggest YouTuber in the world. For all the wrong reasons. And today of all days – April Fool's Day. Despite me pleading with ToolBot not to put up the video, he's edited it to make me look even more ridiculous and put it on up his channel. He's mentioned me in every single way possible, and it's already been viewed over two million times.

I promised myself I wouldn't read the comments. I feel ridiculous enough as it is, and my phone hasn't stopped beeping all day. It feels like there isn't one person I know who hasn't seen it.

I must not look.

I must not look.

I'M LOOKING.

Great. I'm a laughing stock. Everyone thinks TuBot is some kind of hero and I'm some kind of idiot. It feels like everyone in the universe is talking about me, and the video has started trending on Twitter.

#ladgoals
#TuBotrules
#saffrondoesntgetbants

#ihatethisday

Most people are saying that I can't take a joke or that the video is clearly a total set-up. I don't want to respond, because it will just feed the situation, so all I can do is wait for it to blow over.

I moved to LA to make my mark, but not like this. Be careful what you wish for, eh? The only positive thing is that I've got, like, tons more followers. I've got another 200,000 already. I guess people are waiting to see how I respond.

Steve called me earlier and he's over the moon about the video. He thinks this could help me break America. I mean, it's what I want to do, but not like this.

At home we celebrate April Fool's Day. I love doing stupid stuff to my family. My dad never realizes what day it is, so last year I told him I'd agree to do a glamour shoot for a men's mag, and I swear I saw steam coming out of his ears at one point. My mum played along and we thought it was hilarious.

The best prank I ever played on Casey was covering the toilet with cling film so when he went for a wee it went <everywhere>. He was not impressed, and neither was my mum. Neither was I when I had to clean it up. I held the end of the mop and stayed as far away from the mess as I possibly could. I hadn't thought about the repercussions of the joke.

I think my brothers are worse to me than I am to them, though. And not just on April Fool's Day, all year round. The worst thing Casey's ever done to me was when I'd been away to Amsterdam for work.

I'd had so much fun, but it had been such a busy time. When I got home I was so tired, and all I wanted to do was go to bed. I was actually dreaming of putting on my pyjamas and my eye mask and turning the light out at, like, 9pm. It was so bad, I'd even decided which pyjamas I was going to wear. I've got these ridiculous fleecy ones with rainbows on that are quite old, but they feel like a nice warm hug when I put them on, because they're so cosy. I really needed comfort that day. Instead, what I got was this:

When I got home, I could tell something was up. My mum was looking really shady and Casey was jumping around like something really exciting had happened. I ran up to my room the second I got home, and I noticed there was something on my door handle. When I looked closer I saw it was a balloon, and I was properly confused. I pushed my door. and it felt like someone was stood the other side. Then I heard laughter, and when I opened the door fully I saw that the entire room was full of balloons, and everything – and I mean <everything> – was covered in silver foil. From my light to my desk to my computer to my – oh my god – <my

bed>. I laughed, because I didn't know what else to do, but honestly I wanted to cry. All I could say was, 'What the hell have you done to my room?'

How could Casey do this to me? I wanted to lie down and not move for at least twelve hours, but instead I jumped onto the bed and got swallowed up by a ton of tin foil.

I had to painstakingly peel the foil off my bed and it was so ridiculous. It was so annoying, but I can't help thinking it was probably more annoying for Casey, who spent literally an entire morning doing it.

Casey does really irritating things. Another time, I was arguing with him in the kitchen. He was eating a jam tart, and he turned around and stuck it on my nose and then started wetting himself. I was so cross, because I'd just done my make-up and my nose was all sticky and horrible.

Jed and Casey also used to lock me in a room by putting a chair under the handle outside so I couldn't open the door, which they found <so> funny and I found <so> annoying.

My Safe Place

As anyone who's watched my room tours online knows, my bedroom is everything to me. It's where I can take time and do my work. I film in my bedroom, I edit in my bedroom and I sleep in my bedroom, so I spend more time there than anywhere else. It's a multi-tasking bedroom!

My absolute favourite thing in my bedroom is my bed, because it's so comfy. I love my big, long desk where I can do my work, because as soon as I sit down at it I feel like I'm in the zone.

I moved bedrooms a while ago and I must admit I preferred the position of my old bedroom, because now I'm next to my parents and my mum will bang on the wall and shout at me when my TV is too loud. Which is most nights.

What I keep in my bedside table

I know, I know, it's the question you've been desperate to know the answer to for years. Just what <is> in my bedside cabinet?

- A pen and a notebook for when I want to write ideas down.
- A phone charger.
- A lip balm that's probably about three years old.
- A book I'll probably never read.
- Countless hair bands and hair clips.
- The odd false eyelash.

Now I've given you that fascinating peek into what's in my bedside drawers, it would be weird if I didn't tell you what was on top of them. Wouldn't it? Maybe?

Anyway, on one side there are some photos of me with

some friends and a candle. And on the side there are some photos of me with some friends and a candle. I'm a creature of habit.

What's under my bed?

I'm <so> glad you asked. I've been waiting for someone to ask that question for years. I actually looked the other day and found this:

* A big box of lovely letters from viewers, along with some really cool things people have made me.
* More hair bands and clips.
* Some receipts.
* One of Bella's toys (random).
* An elastic band, even though I haven't used one for years and I have no idea why it's there.

The weirdest dream I've ever had (I know this is a weird link but I dream in bed, and we're talking about my bed)

I had this recurring dream when I was about fourteen. There was this boy called Adrian who I fancied at school, and in the dream we used to turn into mermaids and live happily ever after in the sea. I must have had it at least twenty times. I used to go to bed saying to myself, 'Me, Adrian, mermaid', so I could dream about him again.

Please don't let Adrian see this. In fact, let's change his name to Tristan instead.

My morning routine

I absolutely adore sleeping, and it's always a bit of a shock to have to wake up in the morning. But, actually, I wake up feeling pretty excited about what the day might hold. I've usually got plans every single day and, if I don't, I'll be working on video ideas.

My alarm goes off at around 8.30am, and the first thing I do is check out social media and see what's been going overnight, and catch up on all the things I've missed. I usually go onto Instagram first, and then Twitter to post my morning tweet.

I'll grab my laptop next, and check out my stats and reply to some comments and chat to my viewers. I also go to my subscription box to see what other people are up to, and catch up on videos because I love watching other YouTubers' uploads.

I'll pop on my Ugg slippers and then brush my teeth and wash my face, and then it's time for breakfast. I love cereal too much, and there are days when I literally roll out of bed, open my eyes and have breakfast. I'm really trying not to do it anymore but it's proving <hard>. It's only a matter of time before I install a mini-fridge and kitchen cupboard in my bedroom so I can eat in bed.

Once I've had breakfast, I put my make-up on, which for

some reason I do while I'm sat crossed-legged on the floor in front of my door. I have no idea why I don't do it at my desk, where all my make-up is. It's such a weird habit, and one my mum can't seem to get her head around because she always tries to open the door while I'm sat there.

Next, I'll get dressed because, let's face it, people get a bit funny if you leave the house without doing that. I know, right? People can be so uptight.

Once I've got some clothes on, I'm good to go. I might take Bella out or start working on a new video. Or, if I've got a meeting, I'll get my work head on and off I go.

April 3rd

I've been doing my best to keep my head down for the past couple of days. Leonie has been going out to get us food and then we've been hiding out. I've been trying to avoid being hassled, but somehow people have got hold of my phone number so I've had loads of messages from people asking me for my side of the story. I mean, is it really that big a deal that someone tried to kiss and me then put an ice-cream down my top? Apparently it is.

This massive American website called TMZ wants to interview me, and Steve is desperate for me to do it because he says the exposure will be mind-blowing. But what if they're on ToolBot's side and they make me look even more ludicrous?

There's this whole attitude that 'all press is good press' in LA. But it's not great when everyone is already taking the mickey out of you, and this could add more fuel to the fire. I would rather do it on my own terms when I'm ready, by uploading a video that is straight from my heart and something that people can't take out of context.

I spoke to Mum, and she said that everyone is talking about the video back home too. She also said that these things blow over, and she's right. There will be something else for everyone to talk about next week.

Thankfully, Ryan has been pretty understanding about things. I don't think he's <thrilled> about the whole kiss thing and it was pretty awkward the first time I spoke to him after my #videonightmare but he seems to be okay about it. I guess I'll be able to work out more when I see him, but I'm not sure when that will be.

He doesn't want to come round because he's worried a pap may see him coming into the building, and put two and two together. He's concerned that it will affect his brand if he's associated with me right now, which I do get. He really wants to become a massive model and get loads of campaigns, so he needs to be careful about where he's pictured and stuff. It will be easier to work things out once we can properly talk. Hopefully this will all die down soon.

In the meantime, my subscriber stats have gone crazy. I'm well into the millions now. I think tomorrow will be the right time for me to a) leave the apartment and b) record a video. It's going to be a big day!

April 4th

The video is UP. I didn't go too crazy and make a big deal out of things, I just told the truth. I said really clearly that I didn't ever say it was okay for ToolBot to kiss me (I actually nearly called him that in the video!).

Things have been pretty quiet so far. A lot of people have commented that they support me, which is so nice to hear. I feel like I'm getting a bit of cabin fever, so Leonie and I are going to go out and meet Beth soon. I need to get out and get some fresh air. I can't hide away forever, as much as I have enjoyed watched the entire series of Riverdale *again.*

(Later the same day . . .)

Well, that was a short trip out. I wish someone had warned me there were paps outside. Leonie and I tried to dodge them, but we ended up having to run down the street and then come back into the building the back way. It wasn't that sensible, because now they know that exists they'll probably wait out there too.

They definitely managed to get some photos of me, but I kept my head down as much as possible. In a case of the worst luck <ever>*, I've got a spot on my nose. I just know if any of the paps got a full-on shot of my face, that will be the thing that will end up with a ring around and a massive arrow pointing to it if anyone prints it. They'll probably say it's a stress spot and that the upset of the ice-cream incident has caused my skin to break out. Brilliant.*

Steve phoned me earlier to say he wishes I had run the video past him before I put it up, because he would have made it much more 'dramatic'. The whole thing is dramatic enough as it is! If anything I'm trying to play it down.

I know some people have launched entire careers based on one questionable video, but I don't really want it to be the thing I'm always known for. I know ToolBot is a massive deal over here, but I'd rather not use someone else to get famous. Especially when it involves me looking more ridiculous than I ever have in my entire life.

April 5th

I woke up to this:

> *From: TuBot@imanidiotbutyoudontrealiseyet.com*
> *To: Saffronbarker@themoon.com*
> *Subject: Re: Our cool as f@@k video*
>
> Saffron, I've seen your video and it was not a cool thing to do. How can you deny you agreed to kiss me? I'll be putting up another video later today to set the record straight.

NOOOOOOOO. (Also note no kiss on the end of the email. Not that I wanted one. On an email or otherwise).

April 6th

I'm officially over it. In fact, I'm beyond over it. ToolBot's video has gone viral and my phone has not stopped ringing again. How can this be <so> important?

I have to be the bigger person here. I have to pretend like none of this happened and get on with my life. I'm going to carry on vlogging and uploading videos like I always have, and wait for it to go away. Maybe if I ignore this, everyone else will. It sucks.

April 10th

Things seem to finally be calming down. I've realized that if I keep replying to ToolBot, he'll just keep coming back at me and it will never stop. All I can do is look at the positive, and that is that I now have a massive following and I can use it for good. I'm going to make this experience as positive as possible.

I've been venturing out a lot more and the weird thing is that, after several months of no one knowing me out here, total strangers have been coming up and chatting to me. I'm used to getting recognized when I'm out and about in the UK, but it feels very different when someone comes up to me in New Look to say hello than when it does when someone stops me as I'm checking out the Hollywood Walk of Fame.

Honestly, people have been so nice and I've been getting a lot of love. I feel like things are starting to go back to normal. Well, as normal as they get in my world.

I love chatting to new people, but I don't always know how to actually start a conversation. I go to lots of events where sometimes I don't know anyone, so I have no choice but to start talking to random people and hope for the best!

I usually start out by saying, 'Are you from around here?', which I know is really lame but it always seems to be the first thing that comes into my head! Sometimes I'll ask them about something they're wearing because that always breaks the ice.

If I get nervous, I have a habit of saying that everything is 'cool' or 'awesome'. Like, someone will say they got the train that day and I'll say, 'That's awesome' when it's really not. Since when was getting a train awesome? Unless you're in first class and Brooklyn Beckham is sat opposite you.

I also tend to ramble loads. I lose track of what I'm saying and I'm not even sure I'm making sense half the time.

The weird thing about meeting new people is that they know loads about me from my vlogs, but I don't know anything about them. People will say, 'How is Bella? Is she doing okay?' And I'm thinking, 'This is weird. I can't ask you how your dog is because I don't know if you've got one.'

It's strange that people know a lot about my life. This is an actual conversation I had with someone recently:

Me: 'Hi, how are you?'

Other girl: 'I'm really good thanks. How is your mum? How is Casey doing? Have you tidied your room up? It looked a bit messy on your video the other day.'

Me: 'My mum's really well thanks. So is Casey. My room's still messy, though, annoyingly.'

Other girl: 'Oh, cool.'

(Thought bubble: 'Oh no, what do I ask her about? I don't know her mum. I don't know if she's got any brothers. And I've never seen her bedroom.')

Me: 'Are you from around here?'

I suppose I do put my whole life out there, so people think they know me really well. I just need to think of some really good questions to ask back that don't require me to know anything about them!

April 26th

I still haven't seen Ryan. He's been really keeping his distance since the ToolBot drama. We've still been messaging a lot and he keeps saying he wants to meet, but every time I suggest we do something, he backs off again. It's so confusing. Like, you're either interested or you're not. I would much rather guys were clear-cut about things.

I have had some really cool news, though. I've been invited to a film premiere at Grauman's Chinese Theatre. It's a really famous cinema on the Walk of Fame, and apparently loads of stars are going to be there. I really hope one of the Kardashians is going. I must be the only person in LA never to have seen one of them. I missed Kim by, like, five minutes on Rodeo Drive the other day, and I was so upset.

This is going to be the first Easter I've ever spent without my family, but Leonie, Beth and I are going to have dinner together at a place called Fig & Olive, on Melrose. It looks really nice, and I've checked and it's got chicken on the menu. It won't be quite the same as having a roast at home with my family, but at least we'll get to celebrate.

I love Easter because everyone gets time off, so I have a chance to see more of my friends and family. I always see it as a really happy time. If the weather is good, we'll all sit outside in the garden, or sometimes we'll go for a walk on the beach.

My family usually has a bit of a get-together and an Easter

egg hunt. My granddad will buy lots of plastic eggs – mine are always pink, Jed's are yellow and Casey's are blue – and then he'll hide them around the house, and we have to find them. He'll put mini-chocolates and money in them (not loads, but when you've got fifteen eggs the money mounts up!), and then at the end there will be a big Easter egg for each of us. I love it.

Our family get-togethers are always very loud and very fun, and everyone goes a bit crazy. We always seem to have them at our house, and my aunties and uncles and grandparents pile over, and everyone mucks in and helps out.

Even though we don't see each other loads, we're all very close. We're very alike and we're not afraid to be honest with each other. I lose count of the number of times people shout, 'I can't believe you've just said that!' across the dinner table.

Our gatherings are hilarious, and people love seeing them on my vlogs. My mum and her two sisters are so ridiculously similar and their kids are just like me, Jed and Casey, so it's so fun when we all get to hang out. Someone will always be playing guitar, and someone else will be singing along way too loudly. My auntie fell off a Segway in the background of one of my videos in front of everyone once, and we just carried on as if nothing had happened. You know, like it's the most normal thing in the world.

It's so laid-back and easy, and no one gets offended if

someone wants to do a runner at the end of the evening. We don't have to do that whole polite goodbye thing. Sometimes, people will literally just get up and walk out, and it will take half an hour for us to notice they've properly left!

People on YouTube are like, 'What even are your family?' And I can understand why. We are funny to watch. If someone were to write a sitcom about my family, it wouldn't be anywhere near as funny as the real thing.

CHAPTER 5

May

May 2nd

I finally saw Ryan again today. It was the first time in over a month, and we arranged to meet in our favourite coffee shop. He came dressed in a cap and some sunglasses, which was, like, so weird. Usually people are staring at me like, 'That's that girl from TuBot's video', but actually today everyone was looking at him because he looked like he was some big-time celebrity trying to disguise himself. I can only think he's still worried about being seen with me, which doesn't feel great, TBH. Surely you either want to be with someone or you don't?

I'm going to see how Ryan behaves over the next few weeks, but if things don't get better, I don't think I've got any choice but to break up with him. I really like him, but let's face it, it's pretty hard to have a proper relationship with someone who seems embarrassed to be seen with you.

I thought I was going to be with my ex forever, but sometimes what you think is going to be isn't going to be. Simple as that. When we split up, I was devastated. I cried for days and I let myself feel really rubbish. Then I picked myself up and got on with life, because you have no choice but to do that.

It all came about because he wasn't replying to any of my messages and I was really confused. We'd spent the first year and a half of our relationship being so happy and we never, ever argued. Then things started to go downhill, and we were bickering so much I did think it would never get back to where it had been. Alarm bells started ringing, and of course I knew something wasn't right when he stopped getting in touch. Things hadn't been going very well for a while and he'd changed a lot. I didn't want it to carry on if it wasn't what we both really wanted, so I ended up finishing with him by text.

He replied, 'Yeah, I think it's for the best', and it was

such a cold reply, I even wondered if someone else had written it for him. It wasn't like him at all. You wouldn't be that black and white about it after being with someone for two years, unless something else was going on. And, as everyone knows, sadly he did something that completely broke my trust. I don't know if he was being off with me because he felt guilty, but he didn't act like the person I knew at all.

I was so upset, I didn't think I'd ever stop crying. My friends and family really helped me to get through it and told me I was going to be okay. They were really there for me, and my friends Georgie and Libby were amazing. Even mates I hadn't see that much rallied round, and that meant the world to me.

It made it so much harder that everything happened in the public eye. I couldn't get away from him, because I was always seeing him on social media and his videos were always popping up on YouTube.

Everyone was watching and judging every single thing that we both did, and it was a horrible time. Once you've had your heart broken, it's hard to trust guys again.

Mum was almost as sad as I was when we broke up. Not because she missed having my ex around, because she was furious with him, but because she hated seeing me so upset.

She acrually cried when she saw how heartbroken I was. She even said to my dad, 'I don't know how I'm going to fix her heart.' 😢😢😢😢

Viewers kept asking me about what happened and, if I ever did talk about it, other people would be like, 'Stop bringing it up again.' But I honestly didn't answer a fraction of the questions I was asked, and I actually kept really quiet about it. I could have said a lot of stuff, but I didn't, because I still respected my ex despite everything, and I really hoped he would do the same. We had cared about each other a lot, and there was no need for us to start slagging each other off. I didn't want people to take sides and hate him or hate me, because there was no need.

I had to kind of accept the situation and make the best of it.

People always said to me, 'How did you stay so positive throughout everything?' and honestly, it was an effort at first. I knew we weren't ever going to get back together, so all I could do was make the best of it.

I won't say it wasn't difficult, because sometimes it really was. I missed us as a couple, because we were always making nice plans and doing cool things together. The thing that was most upsetting was that he'd also been my best friend. I'd seen him so much when we were together that I didn't see my other friends as much as I used to, and because we were both doing YouTube, we had tons in common. I felt like I'd I lost my boyfriend and my best friend at the same time.

But slowly but surely I began to feel better. In the end, it was actually anger that got me through the heartbreak. Anger is a much stronger feeling than sadness, and I was so hurt by what he'd done to me, it kind of drove me on to feel better. Then, once the anger went, I felt pretty okay again.

In a way, my ex did me a favour, because how he behaved meant I got over him much more quickly than I would have done if it had been different. Although I was so upset, actually it worked out for the best, because I felt like I had an opportunity to make a new start.

Even now, people say how different I am to when I was with him. I don't really see it, but I guess I've also grown up a bit over the last year, so I'm different in that way too. I'm more independent and probably more myself. I'm not one half of a couple of anymore. I'm just Saffron.

Everything happens for a reason, and I wouldn't want to go back and change anything about our time together. It was great while it lasted, and we had some really, really fun times together. At least I've got a lot of nice memories of us, and they're what I focus on, not the rubbish bits.

My top five tips for moving on from a break-up

1) Remember that how you feel after the break-up isn't how you're going to feel in a month's time.
2) Spoil yourself. Properly pamper yourself and buy yourself a present lots of presents.
3) Flirt! Because you can again!
4) Don't think of it as the end of something; think of it as the beginning of a new phase.
5) Remind yourself how totally incredible you are.

It's weird meeting new guys now, because they often know quite a lot about me and I don't know a single thing about them. They could pretend to be anyone they want, whereas my life is pretty much all online, so I can't get away with anything!

When I meet the right person, of course I'll take a chance on them, but I'll probably take things pretty slowly. I don't think I'd be brave enough to ask a guy out if I like him. Maybe I would suggest that we hung out sometimes, but I'd try and be subtle about it. Which I'm generally not.

May 10th

It's red carpet day! I'm not joking, I've spent four days trying to decide what to wear. In the end, Leonie and I went shopping today and we found the cutest shop. They only had one of every dress in stock, so hopefully that will mean no one else will be wearing the same thing.

It would be the dream to have designers dressing me one day. I know that loads of the really big stars have clothes literally thrown (okay, maybe not literally) at them. Apparently, all the stylists have to make 100 per cent sure that no one else is going to be wearing the same thing as the person they're dressing. If two people turn up in the same outfit, it means instant sacking for everyone involved. That is <way> harsh, but I'll never forget how embarrassed I was when I turned to my friends eleventh birthday party wearing the same dress as her, so I do kind of get it. Cringe!

Leonie has such cool taste, and it's always good to have a second opinion. Usually, my mum would be there with me, helping me to make a decision, but I did FaceTime her when I got home to show her what I'd picked out and it met with her approval! I chose a long, green, backless dress that has all a diamanté trim all around the bottom, so it sparkles when you walk. You can't even see it unless you're moving but it really catches the light, which will look amazing if anyone takes my photo. I'm not expecting paps to be exactly fighting each other to get a shot of me when there will be proper A-listers there, but you've always got to be prepared, just in case.

I know they always have <tons> of photographers at those kinds of events. I just hope people don't recognize me as 'the TuBot girl', and try and get a picture of me tripping over or something. I'm hoping this time, I'll get in the press for the right reasons.

Beth came over and did my hair and make-up for me before I left home. I was super excited to try and find out who else was going to the premiere, so we started Googling to check out who is in town. Zac Efron is away filming, annoyingly, but Brooklyn Beckham is definitely around because he was papped at Soul Cycle (literally the coolest gym in the world) yesterday.

I filmed a really long vlog while I was getting ready and Leonie, Beth and I were laughing the whole way through. I'm sure they were just as excited as I was.

I can't believe how cool Leonie's been with me. I am paying her to stay in her apartment, obviously, but she makes me feel like it's my place too. I always used to imagine what it would be like to live with friends, and this is even better than I hoped. I think because she's a few years older than me, she sort of looks after me too.

The only thing we don't agree on is Ryan. She thinks he's a bit of a player, and she doesn't like the way he goes off radar all the time. I've explained that he gets super busy with work and that he found the TuBot nightmare tough to deal with, but she reckons he's being selfish.

I can see where she's coming from because I feel a bit up in the air about things at times. But then when I see him he's <so> lovely to me, and we have a real connection. He bought me this lovely anklet from one of my favourite stores in LA. It's a real hippy shop, and everything is handmade by the owner. It was so sweet and thoughtful, and I literally died when he handed it over.

Beth has been so kind to me since I've been out here too. She's originally from Texas and her accent is <everything>. It's the cutest thing. She moved to LA because she wants to be a make-up artist on movie sets, and I can totally see it happening. She's so talented. Her portfolio is full of beautiful pictures of models she's worked with. She's got this other section that's full of theatrical photos. She's working on a low-budget zombie film at the moment, and I swear she's based one of the looks on how Casey looks when he gets in from a night out with his friends.

Beth's given me some really great advice about being away from home, and she told me that she missed her family so much when she first moved away. She's lucky because her flight home is only a few hours, whereas mine is over eleven. I was a bit teary the other day, because I saw a photo Casey put up on Twitter of the family having dinner. Beth asked why I didn't go home for a visit. But honestly? If I did, I'm not sure I would come back. I'm not even halfway through my LA year yet, and I've still got SO much to do.

I do get pretty nervous when I'm going to big dos. Because it's such a selective event (I know, check me out), I'm not allowed to take anyone with me, so I'll be flying totally solo. So obviously I'll be rolling out my killer conversation lines to a bunch of total strangers. Wish me luck!

May 11th

I literally cannot believe what happened last night. I'll start right at the beginning, so I don't miss out a single detail.

My Uber picked me up from the apartment at 7pm. I was due to be on the red carpet at 7.30pm and the venue is only ten minutes away so I thought I had <tons> of time. I didn't count on early evening LA traffic though.

I was panicking so much, I kept reapplying my lipstick to keep myself calm. Don't ask me why. I have no idea why I thought it would help, but by the time I arrived at the theatre, I was so stressed and I looked like I'd had some serious fillers.

I literally ran out of the car and over to the nearest woman with a clipboard and introduced myself.

'Ah yes, Saffron. Hi,' she said, without looking up.

'I'm really sorry. The traffic was terrible and—'

Before I could say anything else, she put her finger to her lips and walked off, expecting me to follow her. She was clearly a woman of few words.

She asked me to stand in front of the promo board (basically a giant board that had the film's title written across it about 100 times) to have my photo taken. Then she pointed to the beginning of the red carpet. And that's when it all went horribly, horribly wrong.

I stood still for a minute so the bank of paps could take my picture and, as the flashbulbs started pinging, I looked around to see which celebs I could spot. There were loads of people further up the carpet, signing autographs for fans, but because of the reflections of the camera lights, it was hard to focus.

Then I saw him. Brooklyn Beckham. Even with a bad case of flash blindness, I knew I wasn't mistaken. My future husband was just feet away from me. I started walking up the red carpet, way too fast for someone who was trying to act cool, and I was just about to introduce myself when I saw a figure heading towards me out of the corner of my still slightly dazzled eye.

'Hi Brooklyn. I, erm, just wanted to say hello,' I said to the back of Brooklyn's perfectly fitted suit jacket.

At the very moment he turned around to face me, I heard a noise and watched in slow motion as TuBot lunged at me, planting a massive kiss on my cheek, much to the delight of all the paps. HOW CAN THIS BE HAPPENING?

THIS IS NOT MY LIFE.

I'M NOT HERE.

I'M DREAMING.

I'M GOING TO WAKE UP ANY MINUTE.

I WANT TO CRY.

'BABES! How are <you>? It's been <too> long,' shouted TuBot at the top of his voice, trying to gain the maximum attention possible.

I looked desperately at Brooklyn and watched as he smiled sympathetically. Then, out of nowhere, an overzealous PR swooped in and moved him down the carpet to another group of journalists. And that was it. My chance was gone.

Once he'd milked the photo op for all it was worth,TuBot went bounding back to his adoring public and I was left standing on my own in total shock.

I'd been well and truly set up.

I spent the rest of the evening trying to avoid TuBot. Thankfully, I wasn't sat next to him in the cinema or anything, and the minute the film was over I jumped straight into a *cab home. Not even the sight of Ryan Seacrest (and someone who used to be in *NSYNC but wasn't Justin Timberlake) could lure me to the aftershow party.*

I literally love going to red carpet events, but there is always a risk that something is going to go wrong. There are so many opportunities for fails!

I went to LA for an event for Nickelodeon in early 2017, which was amazing. Although the red carpet was actually orange that day. Everyone was so glamorous, and I wore this dress I loved that only cost me £15 online. The funny thing is that so many people asked me where it was from.

Everyone else was in these $1000 dresses and I was there in this cheap number. And I'm not someone who can lie about stuff like that. Every time someone asked me about it I was like, 'Yeah, it was only £15!' Which is the equivalent of about $25.

It helped that I was wearing my mum's designer shoes. I'd forgotten to pack my own shoes – complete crisis – so I'd borrowed her super high Louboutins. I felt like I was on stilts, and even though they were only half a size too big, they felt massive.

I'd love to say I've got some tips for walking in heels, but I've got <nothing>. My tactic is to hope for the best and keep moving. Someone told me once you should 'always trust the heel' on a shoe and know that they'll support you, i.e. don't lean forward like so many women do when they're scared of falling over. I don't know if that works, but it sounds like pretty good advice.

I spent the whole time squeezing the front of my feet just to try and keep the Louboutins on. My feet were getting so sweaty, and considering how high the shoes were I felt like I was doing really well even walking in them. Even my mum can only wear those shoes for a couple of hours at a time. I felt so proud. (I can't even tell you how good it felt to get them off at the end of the night. I'm not great in heels at the best of times, and imagine if I'd stacked it in front of all those cameras?)

Just before I was about to walk out in front of the photographers, I started talking to some fellow YouTubers called Jess and Gabriel. They were so lovely and we were chatting away like we'd known each other for ages. They really helped me with my nerves. Mum was with me, but she waiting in the green room, so I was totally alone and feeling a little bit vulnerable.

So, there I was hanging out with my new BFFs when this guy from Nickelodeon came over to introduce himself. As he did, I heard Gabriel turn to Jess and whisper something about me. I heard my name really clearly and I could feel my face going, like,<bright> red. Maybe we weren't BFFs after all? Maybe Gabriel was saying how annoying I was? (Not that I was feeling paranoid or anything.)

The guy from Nickelodeon left, and I started feeling so uncomfortable. I was thinking, 'Should I say something to Gabriel? Should I not? Should I side step away like a crab in the hope they don't notice?' It was properly awkward.

'Saffron,' said Gabriel.

This was it. This was the moment he was going to ask me

to go and stand somewhere else so I didn't cramp his and Jess's style.

'I hate to say this,' he continued (never a good conversation opener). 'The thing is . . . I know, if I was a girl, I'd want to know too. Erm. You've got lipstick on your teeth. I don't want you to be offended but I had to tell you.'

I nearly hugged him. I was so <not> offended. I was about to walk out in front of a hundred thousand cameras. Imagine if I'd had bright-red teeth in all the photos? <So> cringe.

I think, in those instances, it's totally fine to come clean to someone if you're trying to help them out. It's very unlikely you'll offend someone if you're just trying to do them a favour. It's less offensive to tell someone than <not> to tell them.

My mum is so militant about that kind of thing, she'll tell a stranger walking down the street if they've got a price label hanging out of their top. I'm not quite that brave yet, but I think it's a really cool thing to do. I would want someone to let me know.

I totally did that classic thing of having my skirt tucked in my knickers after a PE class once. I was rushing to get to lunch and I got dressed so quickly I didn't realize. I was about to run out of the changing rooms, and one of my friends was like, 'NOOOOOO, SAFFRON! STOP!' I was so grateful.

Another time, I was walking around with toilet roll stuck on my shoe for ages and I had no idea. That is one of the least cool things you can ever do. It was even worse because this really cute boy started walking towards me and I was like, 'He-llo there'. Then he smiled at me really nervously and said, 'Just to let you know, you've got a massive bit of loo roll trailing behind you.' <Great>.

Advice time!

How do you tell a friend something they might not appreciate? Carefully, unless you know them super well. You don't want to upset or hurt anyone.

You have to know how far you can go with what you say with different people. One of my friends is really sensitive, so if I told her she had lipstick on her teeth, she'd literally be so offended. No joke. Like, she'd probably cry, even though you're saying it for her benefit. Whereas other friends love a bit of tough love, and they would never get upset, whatever I said.

If someone asks me for an honest appraisal of something, I'll always start my reply with, 'In my opinion . . .' so it makes it really clear that they're allowed their own opinion too!

I also copy Gabriel's approach now and say, 'I don't want to offend you and I'm only telling you this because I would want to be told.'

If ever someone asks for my opinion on an item of clothing and I'm not keen on something I'll say, 'Well I wouldn't wear it, but it might look good on you.' Because, at the end of the day, it might!

(Not if it's really ugly. There are some things that don't look good on anyone).

If you're ever in doubt, think about how you'd feel if the roles were reversed. Would you be happy for someone to tell you if you had a twig sticking out of your topknot if front of other people? Probably. Would you be as happy if they told you your breath smelt like you'd eaten the garlic section of Sainsbury's? Er, no.

I called Steve to tell him what happened at the premiere and strangely he didn't seem in the least bit shocked.

'Ha! I guess it was quite a surprise?' he said.

'Yes,' I replied. 'A massive one. Hang on, did you know about it? Were you the one who set this up?'

'Honey, you were the one who said you want to be make it BIG,' he laughed. 'I'm just giving you a nudge in the right direction.

'Brilliant. Thanks, Steve, but there's a big difference between making it big and looking like a massive idiot.'

May 16th

Thankfully, the fallout from the premiere wasn't as bad as I expected. The pictures were printed on a few websites, and obviously ToolBot made an attention-grabbing video that he uploaded as soon as he got the chance (his shady mate must have been filming it again). But it's not the end of the world.

I'm beginning to get pretty resilient to people calling me 'boring' for not thinking ToolBot's pranks are the most hilarious thing <ever>.

I am grateful I've got more subscribers thanks to the videos – every cloud and all that – but I'm so glad things have died down a bit. Being the most talked about thing on YouTube was kinda cool for a little while, but it was also a lot of pressure.

I think if things ever got, like, super huge, it would be so much harder to keep up with my subscribers. The extra views are great, but I would hate to start worrying about what I posted. I don't ever want to become one of those YouTubers who overthinks things and analyses how people might react if I do something wrong.

To be fair, things always go wrong in my videos. It would be weird if my bedroom wasn't messy or I didn't have a member of family randomly waving their arms in the back-

ground. It does actually feel weird that that hasn't happened for a while. I wonder how my bedroom is? I wonder if Jed has tried to move in there or if Mum's nicked all my make-up?

I was really cross with Steve after his part in the red carpet set-up, and I was seriously thinking about ditching him as a manager (I'm not sure how that would work with the airtight year-long contract I signed, but hey). Then, out of the blue, he called me up and said I had an audition for a new beauty line in early June and, if I got it, it would mean <big> money and <big> exposure. He didn't have many details but it sounded positive.

This is when summer officially starts for me. I always loved this time because it meant that school was almost over, and that was the best news ever.

I hated school more than anyone I've ever known. Literally, the only thing I liked about it was going into town with my friends just before a new term started and picking out a new pencil case and rubbers and pens. Oh, and also . . . Nope, that's it.

I had nice friends, but I was never interested in sitting in the playground looking at boys or slagging off other people.

I thought there were much more interesting things to do.

I'll hold my hands up and say that I'm not academic. Every time I had a science or maths class, I'd think, 'This is a waste of time for me', because I wanted to be at home singing or working on my vlogs. Those subjects are really important for people who want to become scientists or accountants, but I knew that was never going to be my path. I'd get frustrated, because it was such a waste of time and I could have been doing something much more productive and geared towards what I wanted to do long term.

The teachers didn't understand the whole social media thing at all, and some of them were just as bad as the kids when I first started YouTube. They'd say things like, 'What's your future going to be? You can't do YouTube forever you know. You're never going to get anywhere doing that.'

Funnily enough, they did a total 180 by the time I left school and they actually became really supportive, because they could see how well it was going for me. It's a shame people can't be supportive <before> you've proved yourself.

I guess it was all so new, my teachers hadn't come across students doing stuff like that before. They're from a different generation, they don't understand social media as much and what a huge impact it has on people. I don't think they understood that people can actually make money from it and do it long term.

They were sceptical that it would last, and one of my tutors even called YouTube a 'flash in the pan'. But it will always be around. And if anything does happen and it suddenly implodes, I'll find something else I love, because this kind of thing opens the door to lots of other opportunities. No one says you have to do the same thing for the rest of your life, and we've all got choices, haven't we?

I get that my teachers were just trying to give me an education, but I definitely rebelled. I learnt some really helpful stuff at school, but I don't think I'm going to use anything I learnt in my physics class, unless I suddenly decide I want to become the next Stephen Hawking. To be fair, I can't see that happening anytime soon.

School was such a weird time. I liked drama and dance, and that's about it. I was awful at sports, science and maths. I did pass my exams with extra tuition, I had this last-minute burst of working really hard and thankfully I got my qualifications.

(Casey: It is surprising, considering you're so lazy.)

(Saffron: Like you can talk!)

I found my exams so stressful, and I dreaded going into each and every one. Some people are super confident about that kind of thing, but I just wanted it to be over so I could concentrate on what I really wanted to do.

Some people I know actually <enjoyed> exams. How do you even do that? That's like saying you'd enjoy being bitten by a shark or falling over in front of a massive crowd of people and flashing your knickers.

My grammar used to be so bad and, no matter how hard I tried, I just couldn't get my head around spelling and commas and things. I used to laugh about the stupid things I wrote, because it was the only way I knew how to deal with it. I was embarrassed, but I didn't want anyone to know. Then, just before I left school, one of my teachers told me she thought I was dyslexic and should probably have had a test for it several years ago, which makes a lot of sense.

It's frustrating, because if I'd got the help I needed early on, things could have been a lot easier. I can't go back and change it now, but I have had to work really hard to teach myself the basic grammar rules that people take for granted. It's been worth it, but it hasn't been easy.

As I've mentioned before, I didn't talk about YouTube with my friends at school. Apart from a couple of good friends, no one asked me about it, so I kind of got the hint that they weren't interested.

As soon as I was out of school every afternoon, I could do what I loved again and I could talk about it as much as I wanted to with all my YouTube mates. I guess that made me feel accepted, because I didn't follow the crowd at all at school. I sometimes felt like I didn't properly fit in, but it didn't upset me or anything, because not everyone does. And isn't it better to do what you love and make yourself happy, than do what everyone else loves to try and make them happy? I'd sit in school each day knowing that the next seven hours weren't going to be a lot of fun. But then I could disappear into YouTube land.

Loads of my friends were always really excited about getting back to school after we'd had a holiday so they could see everyone and catch up. But not me! Of course I liked seeing my mates, because I loved being with them, but the buzz wore off once I had to go to a Spanish class (my absolute worst thing).

I didn't even enjoy break times. I would much rather have worked through my lunch and gone home early, which people found so weird, because lots of school kids lived for lunchtime.

Most people spent break time gossiping, but I found that so boring. It's such a waste of energy being bitchy about other people. I'd block a lot of it out or walk away if it started. Having said that, if they were slagging off someone who was a friend of mine, I wasn't afraid to stand up for them. I would never agree with something that was being said about someone else if I didn't think it was true, even if it did land me in trouble.

I was always that person who would speak up for others. I'm not saying that to sound like a do-gooder, it's just the way I was. I'm still like that now, and I would never, ever sacrifice my loyalty to a friend just so I could get on the right side of someone.

One time, a girl who was known to be a bully threw food at a friend of mine in the middle of the canteen. It was literally just because my friend was more popular than her and the bully didn't like it. My friend was so upset but no one said a word, not even the boys who were most likely to react. I was the only person who stood up and said it was wrong, and I didn't care if there was a backlash. I didn't want my friend feeling like no one had her back.

If anyone was ever bitchy to me, I could stick up for myself, but half the time I couldn't be bothered because it was wasted energy. Not everyone is going to like everything you do, and I'm fine with that. I think because I always wanted to do me for me, I didn't mind that people didn't love everything I said and did. Being popular has never been the most important thing to me. Being authentic is. I had my friends, and that was enough.

If people didn't like me because I made YouTube videos, that bothered me even less. At the end of the day, they didn't actually know me, and I'm cool with them having an opinion. It would bother me if someone who knew me really well didn't like me, but someone who's made a decision based on a few things they've watched? Not so much. That's their issue, not mine.

I definitely wasn't the best student ever. I got chucked out of class so many times for being on my phone. In the end, I learnt how to text without even looking at it. For that one thing alone, school was invaluable. There may have been the odd word that was wrong here and there, but generally my texts were really on point. My mum would get a message from me at, like, 11am and think, 'How is Saff sending this? She should be in class.' Little did she know . . .

I used to use the school computers to look up clothes I wanted when I should have been working, and it got so bad, they started blocking certain shopping websites. They'd shut my tab down every twenty minutes, so I'd have to start all over again and that was so annoying. It was funny, because they wouldn't ever actually tell me off. They'd just shut down my pages and give me evils across the room.

So many people in my year were absolutely gutted when school finished, but I literally wasn't in any way. Although, I did enjoy my actual last day.It was on May 28th 2016, and I woke up feeling happy. I genuinely had a smile on my face. Apart from having to go back for a few exams the following month, my school days were officially over and done with.

It was a really nice sunny day, and also a pretty busy one. Everyone got their tops signed, we had our leavers' assembly and we also had our group photo taken. I felt kinda weird that I would never be running around the playing field again, and I knew I would miss a lot of people, but the positives of leaving way outweighed the negatives.

My mum, Nicole and I went to Nando's that evening, and then all my mates and I had a party to celebrate the fact we'd never having to go to another physics class again. It was the perfect way to wave my school days goodbye.

CHAPTER 6

June

June 2nd

The weather in LA is amazing right now. It's so sunny and beautiful. It kind of is most of the time, to be fair, but I think because it's June I feel like I want to go declare it's summer and go down to the beach all the time. But I need to stay focused. The audition for the beauty brand is next week, and the last thing I want to do is turn up with a bright-red, sunburnt nose. If I do go out in the sun, it's factor 50 <all> the way.

June 6th

Ryan invited me over to his tonight, so he could cook me dinner. It was, like, <so> weird seeing his apartment after all this time. I half expected him to live somewhere really awful, because I thought there was a reason he hadn't invited me before, but it was way cool.

It had loads of glass and really sleek furniture and an open-plan kitchen and living room, which I think is the ultimate. I really want one of those one day. I plan to be an amazing cook, so I need to be able to whip up amazing creations in the kitchen while my guests chill on the sofa and chat to me.

I think I'm really good at cooking, but actually I'm really not. No hang on, I'm really good at cooking cakes.

(Mum: 'That's called baking, Saffron.')

Okay, I'm really good at baking then.

(Mum: 'Saffron, that's an exaggeration. You use those box mixtures where you just have to add water.')

Not true. Jordan and I made some ginger biscuits once. They were so hard you couldn't eat them, but if no one had tried them we would have got away with it because they looked and smelt really good.

I made an amazing cake with my friend Gee the other day too. We put crushed-up Oreos on the top and it was amazing.

I've never cooked an actual dinner though, apart from one I made once for my ex. I cooked him steak and chips because it was his favourite, but he didn't actually eat any of it, so I don't think Jamie Oliver will be fearing for his job anytime soon.

I think it's probably for the best that I don't cook, considering I once blew up a teddy in the microwave. It was one of those ones you heat up like a hot water bottle. I left it in there for too long and it exploded. If I can blow up a heated teddy, imagine what I'd do if I had to deal with actual food.

Expectation vs reality

Because sometimes things just don't turn out how you expect them to . . .

Cooking

Expectation: I'm going to be a natural!

Reality: I don't think I've ever made anything that's actually edible.

High school

Expectation: I thought I'd go to high school and feel like a grown- up.

Reality: I didn't! I just felt like a kid in a different uniform! You also go from the being the oldest in the school to the youngest. You think you're going to be treated like an adult, and you're so not.

Photoshoots

Expectation: I'll go thinking it's all going to be really glamorous, and I'm going to stand in front of a wind machine looking like Beyoncé.

Reality: I do not look like Beyoncé. My hair will end up in my mouth, and my eyes will start watering so my mascara will stream down my face.

New Year

Expectation: I'm going to wake up feeling different, and it's going to be the best day ever.

Reality: I don't feel any different. Not even a bit.

Starting my period
Expectation: I thought I'd feel like a woman and walk differently and be sophisticated.
Reality: I had period pains.

Online clothes ordering
Expectation: You think you're going to look like the girl in the photo.
Reality: You don't look like the girl in the photo.

My future dream home

My dream home would be really modern, with loads of glass. It would be painted black and white on both the inside and the outside. It would have big gates to keep my matt-black Range Rover safe, and the garden would be perfectely tended to. But not by me. I can't see myself every being someone who enjoys gardening. It's so <messy>.

It goes without saying that I would have a swimming pool, and I'd also have a hot tub, an outside pizza kitchen and a screening room. I want it to be really spacious and I want a huge fireplace in my lounge. I want a place I feel completely relaxed in.

Sometimes I think I'm a bit old before my time, because

there is honestly nothing I love more than getting in after a hard day's shopping and slobbing on the sofa. Don't get me wrong, I do love going out sometimes, but the ultimate for me is lighting a ton of candles (I have so many, it's not even funny) and having a really long bubble bath. I can easily spend an hour in there, especially if I've got some good music on.

Then I'll get into some really comfy lazing clothes, put on my Ugg slippers and either get into bed and watch other people's YouTube videos, or hang out with my family on our crazily comfy sofas. Heaven.

I was seriously impressed by how tidy Ryan's flat was. Maybe he'd cleaned it up to impress me, but it was spotless. Although, sadly, there was one major fail during the evening.

When I arrived, Ryan was already cooking dinner, so I went and talked to him while he was getting it all ready. He knows how much I like chicken (and how many things I <don't> like), so he played it safe and made me chicken with this amazing tomato sauce (no chilli!), roasted vegetables and potato wedges.

After we'd eaten, I thought it would be polite to help out, so I cleared our plates away. When I flipped the bin open to throw our leftovers away – busted! – I saw the take-away cartons in the bin. It's so funny that he'd obviously ordered in, and then taken the food out of the packets and put it into the oven to pass off as his own. What an effort to go to. He could have been honest. I wouldn't have minded.

Personally, I would have been honest about the fact the meal wasn't all my work. If I ever do 'cook' for anyone, my offering will probably come out of a Domino's box.

June 12th

It's audition day again, guys! I'm excited to find out about what the product I'll potentially be modelling is. I'll report back ASAP!

(Later the same day . . .)

I'm going to kill Steve. Honestly, it's going to happen. If you read about a 17-year-old girl who's been arrested for trying to poison her agent, you can safely assume it's me.

That audition was even worse than the last one, if that's at all possible. Don't get me wrong. Steve wasn't lying. The campaign would mean 'massive exposure' – of my blackheads! The company are looking for someone to be the face of their new beauty tool, the Blackhead Blaster – this weird looking metal thing that's supposed to 'rid your face of all that gunk you don't need'! (Great tagline, eh?)

There is no way Steve didn't know what the product was going to be. He told me he was going to come down to have a quick catch-up and see how I got on with the audition, but weirdly he didn't show up.

I went in there with a full face of make-up, ready to impress, and within five minutes the make-up artist had stripped the lot off (I know, ironic when she's a make-up artist) and I was sitting in front of a magnifying mirror while a load of Blackhead Blaster business execs examined my skin to see if they thought I had the right kind of pores.

I swear down, at one point a male exec turned to me and said, 'Do you think your pores would like doing this kind of advert, Sadie?'

My name is Saffron.

Unfortunately, my pores aren't feeling very chatty, so I'll have to come back to you when they're in a better mood.

What even is my life right now?

June 28th

I haven't even bothered to contact Steve to find out whether I got the 'beauty' job or not. Especially as I can't work out if I'll be more insulted if I do or don't get it?

Steve is going from bad to worse. I know I'm not his only client / the most important person in the universe, but come on. The only good thing is that it's given me some really fun content for my vlogs. You literally could not make up a story like that.

I spent such a nice evening replying to comments on YouTube and Twitter, and catching up with friends. I really wanted to connect with the UK because, even though I've got loads of American followers now, I'm realizing more and more that home will always be where my heart is.

I feel like I've been neglecting my YouTube channel recently because I've been mainly vlogging, but it's hard to do challenges and things in Leonie's apartment, because I don't want her to think I'm taking over or making a mess.

Casey is threatening to come over and visit soon, so we can make some cool videos together if he does. Even though we drive each other mad at times, he is the best person to film with. Especially when I win the challenges.

The rules I live my life by

* Always try and beat Casey in challenges.
* Tell yourself you can do something and you can. Believe in yourself and you'll become unstoppable.
* Set yourself goals you know you can achieve and achieve them.
* Always want to do better today than you did yesterday.
* Don't compete with other people.
* Don't be afraid to do something just because you're scared of what people will say about you. People will judge you no matter what.
* Be generous. Not with money, but with what you say. A few nice words can help a person more than you think.
* Don't look back. If Cinderella had gone back for her shoe, she never would have become a princess.
* Be careful who you trust.
* Know that love, laughter and friendship are the best things in life, and they really are free.
* Kindness makes you the most beautiful person in the world, no matter what you look like.
* Always know that the best is yet to come.

* Don't announce on social media that you're going to marry your boyfriend, because there's a chance it may not work out!

(Please note that not all of these quotes are my own. Just because I love a bit of inspo, I honestly don't think I'm some kind of spiritual guru. Sometimes people online say to me, 'You're so inspirational', and I'm like, 'I stole that quote from the internet, but thanks!' But I do fully believe in what all the quotes stand for, and I love a bit of mystical, hippy guidance.)

CHAPTER 7

July

July 4th

I am currently wearing a stars-and-stripes hat, eating fried chicken (it's incredible) and having the best time. It's Independence Day out here, which is when the Americans celebrate their independence, funnily enough. It celebrates the date they broke away from the UK and started ruling themselves.

We're going out to watch fireworks in Long Beach as soon as we've eaten. I've got some new denim shorts and a white cami to wear. And, of course, I'll wear my new hat. Today, I am an honorary American!

July 5th

It's nearly my biiiiiiirthdaaaaaaay! I actually can't believe I'm not going to spend it with my parents for the first time, like, ever. I've never <not> spent a birthday with them. I feel really sad about it, but I'm trying to look at the really positive things in my life so I don't get upset.

I won't see my friends from back home on my birthday, but Leonie and Beth will be here with me.

Ryan called me earlier, and he wants to do something fun to celebrate.

I recorded a really cool YouTube video with Leonie today, which involved us having to having to put make-up on only using things we found in the kitchen. It was messy, we looked awful, but it was hilarious. I keep trying to convince Ryan he should be in a video with me soon, but he still won't say yes. It's so weird, because he's so confident usually!

How to be a successful YouTuber

I honestly started YouTube because I love it, and not for the fame or the money or any of that stuff. I think that's the most important thing. If you're doing it for the wrong reasons, it's going to be much harder to be successful.

Don't worry about having the right equipment, either. Your videos don't have to be perfect. If you can get a camera for your birthday or for Christmas, then brilliant, but don't feel the pressure to spend fortunes on your kit. As long as you film in good light, you don't need tons of filters. Just take the first step and you're on your way!

I bought some really good software early on, which is called Final Cut Pro. It's what a lot of other YouTubers use, because you can do so many things on it and it's really simple to use. My friend Anastasia still uses iMovie and she's really happy with it, so you can totally start with that and just see how you get on.

The best way to get subscribers is to upload at the same time each week and keep to a routine. If you miss doing an upload, people will wonder where you are and you can lose subscribers. It's like when you watch a TV show and you're waiting for the next episode. If it's not there, it's really disappointing, and people feel the same about YouTube.

You can put tags on everything you're talking about on your video. Then, if people are searching for your tag, the video will come up and you'll get more views from that too. Honestly, tag, tag, tag.

Always make videos about what you want and go with

your gut. Viewers always say to me, 'Aww, I love how you always stay positive', but my top five videos are actually the ones where I'm crying, which is so weird! People love seeing how I go from feeling really down to cheering myself up, because it shows another side to me, and I guess then people know they're not the only ones going through hard times.

I've vlogged some really tough, and really personal, things. Last year my mum's best friend, Kerry, died while I was on holiday, and none of us were expecting it. I was so devastated. She was the nicest woman you could ever meet and I'm so lucky she was a part of my life and I was a part of hers. That's one of the most heartbreaking things that's ever happened to me, and it hit me so hard. I also felt so bad for my mum. They'd been friends for so long and they were so close. We will all truly miss her forever, but she will always be with us in our hearts.

It was hard, because I didn't know whether I should mention Kerry's passing in my vlog that day because it was such a private thing. But it was the most significant and life-changing thing that had ever happened to me, so it would have weird <not> to talk about it. In the end, I decided to be open about it, and I'm so glad I did, because the support I got was amazing and it really helped.

Losing Kerry made me realize life can be over so quickly, so you need to make the most of every day and live life to the full. You don't know what tomorrow will bring, but you can try and make it the best day you've ever had.

I don't want to sound like I'm being all self-help-y, but I do want to say that it's okay to be sad. When you're going through something bad, please know you're not the only one, and reach out to people if you need to. The worst thing you can do is not ask for help. And being open and honest really helps too. We all hurt, and that's not in any way weak. If anything, it shows strength if you can share your emotions.

A lot of YouTubers don't show everything and they don't want to put videos of them crying on the internet, but I really don't mind. I think people like the fact that I'm so honest and I'm myself. If they say horrible things, I don't respond. Some people just can't help being mean, and it usually comes from a pretty sad place. No one who is really happy with themselves feels the need to have a go at someone else. They're too busy being fabulous.

When people troll you, they don't think about the fact that you're a human being and that things get to you, so it's good to show that raw side of you and be real about the fact that not everything bounces off of you.

I love being positive, but I also like being <me>. It doesn't matter how famous, good-looking, successful or rich someone is, everyone gets hurt sometimes. Just because someone is well known, it doesn't mean they don't get upset when someone calls them ugly. My life isn't perfect. There, I've said it. I'm as human as everyone else and not everything goes right for me. Especially when it comes to social media.

I vlogged with my friends Harvey and Lauren quite recently. They're both big on social media and we thought it would be cool to get together and do something. I already knew Harvey but it was the first time I'd met Lauren, so I was excited to see how we got on.

We ended up getting having such a laugh, and after we finished the video we were all really pleased with how it went. At least, I was until my mum watched a Snapchat I did straight afterwards and phoned me to ask what I had stuck in my teeth. She said there was this black thing waving out at everyone from the screen, and I had no idea what she was talking about. Then I looked in a mirror and realized I had a bit of raisin stuck in my teeth. It wasn't like it wasn't super obvious either.

The thing is, I'd only eaten raisins for breakfast, so it must have been there all day. I'd travelled to London and back from Brighton on the train, and chatted to loads of viewers, and all the time they must have been thinking, 'Does she know she's got a bit of her breakfast wedged between two of her teeth? Is she trying to start a new trend? Should I mention it or will it make things awkward?'

I was so mortified when I got home and watched the full

video. The raisin was so prominent, it could have had its own YouTube channel. I swear at one point it almost had a breakout moment and started chatting to the viewers.

When the video was uploaded, all the comments on the video were saying things like, 'No true friend would let you do a video without telling you you've got a dead fly in your teeth.' But I honestly think Harvey and Lauren probably felt a bit embarrassed and didn't know how to tell me!

I always have a problem with getting things stuck in my teeth, so I'm always checking them, and since the raisin incident I've been worse than ever. I can't eat a thing without having to get a compact mirror out to make sure no rogue bits of food have been left behind.

My favourite videos of all time

On my main channel, it's my 'I'm a YouTuber' series, because they're funny. It's the first thing I've come across on YouTube that no one else has done.

My favourite vlogs

The Warrior Run that Mum, Dad and I did is one of the best ever because it's so, so fun. And the ones I did at Center Parcs. And the ones I did in Sweden. I reckon travel vlogs are amazing generally because I tend to do my favourite things when I'm travelling.

The most popular vlogs

People love the vlogs I do at home, and they do really well. I guess people like just seeing normal life, and I am very open about mine.

The vlogs I'd happily never watch again

My early ones. They make my cringe so hard. I hate seeing how nervous I was.

The most ridiculous thing that's ever happened on camera
There are three:

1) The time my dad had to wear nipple tassels. I think he secretly liked it. He is really cool about things like that. Like, he'll join in even if I'm making him do something that's a total nightmare, and he'll take it really well.
2) When my dad and I recorded the 'Eat it or wear it' video, I managed to get chilli in my eye. I went off camera and cried because it was so painful, and then I came back on camera smiling and I pretended my eyes were red from the chilli!
3) The time I spent hours and hours doing a Halloween make-up video. Then, at the end, I realized it was terrible and I uploaded it and then took it back down because it was so rubbish. I did not look cool as a mummy with toilet roll wrapped around me. All that work for nothing!

My favourite funny video moments
When I did 'Real food vs gummy food' with Casey, because Casey had to eat an actual scorpion. I like anything that involves other people having to do disgusting things, because it really makes me laugh. I like it any time we get messy or have to do dares.

How I decide what to do in my videos

I'm always coming up with ideas for videos, and my viewers also ask me to do certain things, so I'll take those ideas and put my own twist on them.

How I get people to agree to be in my videos

Simple. I force them. Or I bribe, blackmail or beg them. I actually paid Jed to do a video once. I knew that so many girls fancy him, so I knew they'd love it. I paid him £100, because he wouldn't do it for any less. I tried to negotiate with him for ages, but he wasn't having any of it.

(Casey: 'Hold on, you've never paid me.')

(Mum: 'Or me.')

(Jordan: 'Or me.')

(Dad: 'Or me. We're suckers')

When I realized this YouTube thing was <really> happening

It was when my subscribers hit the 500k mark, because then I started getting recognized double the amount I did before. I couldn't even go on the bus without people knowing who I was, and that was totally crazy.

My AMAZING tips for creating your own YouTube videos (no, really, they are amazing)

- ★ Be yourself. It will be obvious if you're not.
- ★ Don't copy anyone else.
- ★ Make sure the lighting is good. In my opinion, it's more important than having a good camera.
- ★ Write down every single idea you have, no matter how stupid it seems. You can mix it around to make it work.
- ★ Rope your family and friends in as much as possible.

July 12th

I was looking on Twitter earlier, and so many girls are talking about their prom. It's crazy to think mine was a year ago now. I really feel for all the girls who are running around trying to find the perfect dress right now.

This time last year, I was not looking forward to my prom <at all>. I guess because it was so closely linked with school, I couldn't get too excited about it. I left it really late to get my dress too, which didn't help matters. So honestly, anyone who has a prom coming up should do themselves a massive favour and get a dress early, otherwise they'll all sell out. I had a total nightmare.

Mum and I went to London to go shopping and I tried on loads. I found three I loved. I wanted to to somehow merge them all to make my ideal prom dress, but obviously that wasn't really an option. In the end, we went shopping in Brighton and I got an open-backed, diamanté-studded blue dress from a wedding and prom dress shop near me. Then I had to run around manically trying to find the right bra to wear with it, because you could see the straps on all my normal ones. Argh! I also got an amazing silver clutch bag, which went perfectly, and I was so happy about that.

However, my shoes were a different story. I loved them, but they weren't high enough, so I ended up having to take my dress up so it didn't drag along the ground, which added to the last-minute stress. Next time I have to wear a long dress, I'll definitely pick my shoes before my dress, so I'll know they work together.

I woke up really excited on prom day and I went to my friend Claire's house so she could do my make-up. She works for MAC and she's brilliant. I wanted my make-up to really stand out but also look natural, so Claire used some quite muted but dramatic tones. It was such a hot day and I was panicking that my make-up would end up sliding down my face before I even got to prom!

I got my hair done next, and I was quite worried because I hadn't been for a trial. I knew what I wanted to have done, which was a side bun with some bits falling down at the side, but I was also going to a completely new hairdresser, so I had no idea how it would turn out. The hairdresser actually ended up doing such an amazing job, and I grabbed some lunch in the pub next door before I went home to get dressed.

My friends and I got a massive white limo to prom and it was the funniest thing. I ended up having a really good time in the end but the build-up was <such> a drama.

I'm so cross we only get one prom in the UK. American school kids get, like, loads. I think we should have one every year. Then I would have had a chance to properly plan for the big one!

With that in mind . . .

Here are my top prom tips

1) Never, ever put on fake tan the night before prom if you're not used to doing it. You could end up having such a massive fail, and it's hard to get fake tan off. Build

it up over a few days, or use a tinted moisturizer you can wash off.

2) Do anything you can to avoid getting blisters from new shoes. Try and break them in by sauntering around the house in them while wearing one or two pairs of socks (so glamorous). If they're still a killer, rub a stick deodorant on the backs of your heels and it will minimize rubbing. It works, honest.

3) If you're short on time, buy your dress from a shop, not the internet. Trust me, you'll be glad you did. Imagine if the dress turns up on prom day and you hate it? At least if you try it on in advance, you know how it's going to fit and you're not going to be riffling through your wardrobe in a panic, trying to find something that might work.

4) Practise your make-up. Don't go crazy and try to experiment on the day. Because, let's face it, when does that work? Answer: Never. Either stick to what you know or put the hours in beforehand so you know the look you want to go for. There's nothing worse than mascara tears running down your face when you end up looking like you've drawn your face on with kids' crayons.

5) Forgotten to buy false eyelashes? Uh-oh. But all is not lost. For super-thick natural lashes, apply some mascara

as normal. Next, brush your wand over a cotton wool ball until it's covered in fibres. Then brush your lashes, making sure the fibres stick to them. Apply one last coat of mascara and – ta-da! – you'll get instant falsies that won't fall off.

July 23th

The best thing <ever> happened yesterday. I still can't quite believe it. It was one of those times I'll look back at and it will always make me feel so, so happy. No matter how miserable I feel, it will always put a smile on my face.

I was just getting ready to go and vlog in this really cool coffee shop down the road from my apartment, when there was a knock on the door. Seeing as I basically only really know Ryan, Leonie and Beth (and Steve – eurgh) in LA, Leonie always answers the door. But she shouted to me and asked if I could get it.

I opened it, expecting it to be a delivery or something, and my mum and dad were standing there. Like, just <standing> there. I was so shocked, I burst into tears and I couldn't stop crying. They'd flown over to surprise me for *my birthday and I could not have been happier. Leonie had known about them coming, but she'd managed to keep it a secret from me. She was so cute, because when she saw me sobbing with joy, she started crying too! Mum and Dad were in floods.*

'How on earth have you kept this a secret? I only spoke to you yesterday!' I laughed, wiping away my tears with my sleeve (definitely time for a top change).

'You caught us just as we were going out the door,' my mum replied, while also using my sleeve to mop up her tears. 'We had all our suitcases packed and we'd been waiting for the taxi when you called. I had to run into the kitchen so that if the cab arrived, you wouldn't have heard him. The boys and Nicole are at the hotel. They were going to come over and surprise you too, but they're so tired they fell asleep pretty much as soon as we checked in.'

As if this day couldn't get <any> better.

July 24th

My fam have caught up on their sleep and we're off to Universal Studios. Today is going to be ALL about me.

I spoke to Casey last night, and we've planned out a couple of videos we're going to record while we're there, and I can't wait. It somehow feels really normal having them all here. We all usually go away together in July anyway so it's like we're on a family vacation. Only, apart from seeing Mum for a few days in New York, I haven't seen them all for seven months. That has gone ridiculously quickly.

I asked Ryan if he wanted to come with us, but he said he thinks it's too early to meet my parents. I know it's not like we hang out with other every day or anything, but we have been seeing each other for, like, seven months now. That's a pretty long time really. He is <so> weird sometimes.

Casey and I filmed this video where we had to try and blag our way to the front of the queues of rides in the most ridiculous ways possible, and we were killing ourselves. I won, because I told the guy in charge of one of the rides that my hair extensions were really heavy and it hurt to stand up for too long. He clearly felt sorry for me, so he fast tracked me. I can't actually believe it worked. Casey tried to charm a female ride operator by telling her he was related to the Royal Family. But when she asked him what Prince William's daughter was called, he went blank and she busted him. He pretended he 'let' me win because it was my birthday, but there's just no way. My skills were simply too much for him.

I can't wait to put the edit up. I've missed making videos with Casey. I've even missed him. I know. I'm shocked too.

July is one of my favourite months because it always means loads of barbecues, which means <a lot> of chicken. I also see loads of my friends, because they'll have broken up from college, so we'll hang out down at the beach.

I've had some great holidays with my family over the years. We go to Florida a lot, and you can't not have a good time there.

My holidays haven't always been a massive success. I went on another school trip to France when I was younger, but the food they served me was <not> good. Well, I'm sure it would have been great for some people, but I didn't like it <at all>. There was loads of fish, and they even served me mashed potato .

Because I'm so fussy, I didn't eat the whole time I was there, and on the last day we got the chance to go shopping without the teachers for an hour. At the end of the hour, my mates and I stumbled across a McDonald's and I was so excited. I could finally eat something!

We stocked up on tons of food, but by the time it arrived

we were running late to meet everyone back at the coach. We ran all the way, but we were still twenty minutes late and our teacher was in tears because she'd been so stressed. Her tears soon turned to anger, and she grabbed our food and threw the lot in the bin. I swear, it was one of the worst moments of my life. I'd been so excited about my feast and now it was all gone. I'd spent about €16 on it and it was cruelly stolen away from me. What a waste!

I went away to camp with my school the following summer. I stayed with four of my friends, and we had a real laugh. We did loads of activities like canoeing and hiking, and I was loving life.

One day, I was chilling out just outside my tent, and my friend called my name and then threw this china cup for me to catch (I still have no idea why).

It hit the side of my head and this lump came up that was so big I could see it when I looked up. I've always wanted to be a unicorn, and that day my dream came true. It was <massive>. I've never been so embarrassed, and I stayed in my tent for the next two days and cried because it was so painful. I had a permanent headache. Also, every time I ventured out, everyone laughed at me. I don't blame them, because I would have laughed at me too. It was hardly the kind of thing you could cover up with a bit of foundation.

I actually really like camping, but I've mainly gone glamping in the past, so I'm not sure if that counts? I used to go and stay in a caravan with my friends, and I like being in the fresh air and not being on my phone as much. Seriously. The service isn't as good in some places in the country, so I'm kind of forced into a phone detox. Not that I'd be very good if it was a proper one.

The thought of being stranded on an uninhabited desert island for two weeks without my phone makes me feel quite breathless. It's painful to think about it. I'd miss interacting with my viewers, like, so much. I'd miss all social media too.

I'd have to start a fire by rubbing two sticks together and try and send smoke signals to people instead. I wonder if there are emojis for smoke signals yet?

Imagine all the videos I <wouldn't> be able to film! I could ride around the island on the back of a turtle or discover a new animal species, and no one would know about it. How <awful>!

This must never happen. If I ever go off radar and you suspect I've been forced to live a simple life with no technology, please send out a full-on search party. I'm not sure I'd survive.

Having said that, sometimes I look at my phone and I've got so many messages, I feel quite panicked (not actually, I'm being dramatic). And I'm so bad at replying to texts. Unless I reply straight away I totally forget, and then I'll suddenly remember three days later. I always tell my friends to phone me if they need me, because I'm much better with live conversations!

You know how sometimes people advise you to turn off your phone if you want time out to relax and de-stress? Well, not having my phone would make me <more> stressed. I'd be constantly worrying I was missing out on something.

I deleted Twitter once because I felt like I was looking at it too much.

(Mum: 'Saffron, you're making out like you did it for two weeks or something. You barely lasted a day.')

I did actually last a <whole> day. I deleted it one morning, and by 10pm I felt stressed, but I resisted the temptation to go back on it. I woke up the following morning at 9am feeling like I'd had a proper Twitter cleanse, and by 10am I'd downloaded it again. Looking at Twitter is normally the first thing I do, so I thought I'd done really well. Honestly, I was so proud.

YouTube is my favourite thing about social media, without a doubt, but Twitter comes a close second. The interaction is so good, because you get to speak to people directly. I can spend so much time on there and I lose hours. It's like I go into a Twitter black hole and I can't get myself back out. One time, I was looking at my phone for so long that when I looked up, it had got dark outside and I hadn't even noticed.

I'm quite often away on holiday for my birthday, but I always try and celebrate it with as many people as possible. My favourite thing to do is have a nice dinner in the sun or something. I always had parties growing up, and my mum always made them really special, but now I prefer getting a chance to sit down and chat with my mates.

Because my birthday is at the end of July, I'm a Leo, and whenever I read descriptions of my star sign, they seem pretty spot on.

*Apparently we love being centre stage and making an impression, and we're really outgoing and confident, and we like meeting new people.

Yep, yep, yep and yep. As I've mentioned, I've loved performing since I was really young and I'm getting more and more used to being on stage. The more I perform, the more natural it becomes. I also really enjoy getting to know new people, and I always say that strangers are just friends I haven't met yet (hilarious, right?).

*Leos also like holidays, bright colours, fun, friends and attention.

That all sounds about right. Even though my room is pretty much all white, I love experimenting with bright clothes, I love to laugh, my friends mean the absolute world to me and I am not shy when it comes to attention.

I'm pretty upfront about the fact that I'm usually one of the loudest people in a group, although I would hate to be one of those people who doesn't realize they're not giving anyone else a chance to speak. I'll always give other people space to have their say. It doesn't have to be <all> about me!

*We dislike being ignored and people not realizing how great we are.

Ha! This is so funny. I reckon you could probably say this about anyone in the world. Everyone wants people to realize they're pretty great, right? And no one likes being ignored. Why would you like it? What a weird thing that would be.

CHAPTER 8

August

August 1st

My family left today, and I cried my eyes out again. I loved showing them around LA and spending so much time with them. It was so lovely of them to come all this way to see me. I felt guilty, because Jed's literally just finished school and I thought he might want to be at home hanging out with his mates, but he said he's got the rest of the summer to do that, so he's cool.

They've all headed up the coast so they can have a bit of beach time because this will be their big holiday of the year. It's Casey's birthday today, so they'll probably go out for an amazing dinner somewhere. They asked me if I wanted to go with them, but Steve has arranged for me to do another advert audition the day after tomorrow, and this one sounds half-decent!

I've told him that it if involves any kind of spot-removing products, he's in serious trouble. I would honestly rather have to clean Jed's room for a year than go through another experience like my last audition.

But actually, would I? I'm always asking myself questions like this. I often find myself sitting on trains and watching people walk past. I think, 'Where are they going? What are they doing? What's their life like?'

Apparently every single thing we do has a ripple effect on the rest of the world, and it changes things. How weird is that? I think I might think too much sometimes.

The other day I was thinking, what would happen if Bella learnt to talk or if animals took over the world? These are some of the other confusing life questions I'm currently pondering:

Q. Would I rather be a cat or dog?
A. Dog. They're much friendlier. Cats are more independent and go off and do their own thing.

Q. Would I rather eat the world's hottest chilli or a dog biscuit pizza?
A. Dog biscuit pizza. I can't handle any kind of chilli.

Q. Would I rather swim a mile in mud or run twenty miles in rain?
A. I'd swim a mile in mud, because hopefully it would be quicker.

Q. Would I rather go out without make-up or my phone for the day?
A. I'd rather go without make-up. My phone is where I do all my work, so I'd feel so panicked.

Q. Would I rather wear ugly shoes for a month or cut off all my hair?
A. I'd wear ugly shoes. I'd be scared of having really short hair.

Q. Would I rather be mates with Kylie or Kendall?
A. Kylie, because she seems like she'd be more fun.

Q. Would I rather win a year's supply of cereal or a year's supply of crisps?
A. Cereal. I could live on it.

Q. Would I rather be able to see into the future or live in an amazing time in history?
A. I'd go into the future. Hopefully, they would have cured cancer, so I could bring the cure back with me.

August 3rd

Steve has come up trumps! I know! I can barely believe it myself. The audition was for a new hair-curling product, and it was actually really good. One of the casting crew, a lady called Cassie, is a big YouTube fan and she recognized me from ToolBot's videos. I don't know if that's a good thing or a bad thing, but I guess at least she knew who I was, so it wasn't a totally cold audition.

I had to smile into the camera while I was curling a lock of hair and say, 'My curls are <crazy good> when I use the Wunda Hair Wand.'

I said it about twenty times and, in the end, the words stopped making sense! I had to really concentrate to make sure it didn't sound weird. I know it sounds ridiculous, but it was also really difficult trying to curl my hair and concentrate on the line at the same time. I really only like doing one thing at once.

I have no idea if I'm going to get the job because there were a lot of other girls there auditioning, but even if I don't, I actually had a really cool day. Some of the other models (not that I'm a model, but that's what they were calling us – I don't think I'll be chasing Kendall Jenner down a catwalk anytime soon) were so sweet and friendly.

There was one girl there who I was chatting to for ages. She was so pretty and her make-up was a-mazing. We got talking because she was wearing the same anklet as me. Funnily enough, her boyfriend gave it to her too.

I think all the supermodels like Kendall and Gigi and Bella are incredible, and I would literally love to have a night out with them.

If I had been born 6 ft tall and naturally really, really slim, I would love to have been a model. But I'm never going to have that kind of figure. I'm 5 ft 1 and you can tell from looking at me that I'm supposed to have some curves. I'm not a straight up and down kind of girl.

It makes me sad that so many teenagers don't feel good about themselves because they compare how they look to celebrities. Apparently it's getting worse too, and I can totally empathize. I've been through phases where I've wanted to look different, and I've wondered why I don't have Kendall's crazily long legs or Gigi's perfect face. (Random name fact: Gigi Hadid's real name is Jelena Noura Hadid.)

I've spoken before about wanting a nose job because I've got a bump on it, but I really am doing my best to love it. My friends used to call my bump a 'glasses seat' and a 'speed bump'.

I moan about it, but when a friend of mine got hold of a photo of me and she was trying to reshape my nose on an app, I didn't like it at all. It didn't look like me.

I don't mind smoothing out my skin on selfies or whatever, because everyone does a bit of that, but it would be weird if I doctored them to look like someone else, or tried to change myself completely. I am who I am. Bump and all.

It's <crazy> that music videos can be Photoshopped these days. How weird is that? I find that insane. Everyone Photoshops, and I am totally guilty of it, but there's a line. Sometimes I look at pictures of people on Instagram and I can't work out if they're real or if they're a cartoon.

At the end of the day, we're <not> all supermodels, but we deserve to feel like we are. Who says anyone isn't good enough? Waking up and realizing you've got a few spots or your eyebrows suddenly look like sausage dogs doesn't mean you're not as good as you were yesterday. It's a cliché, but it really is what's inside that counts. The people who shine the brightest are the ones who are happy with themselves. No amount of make-up can create that.

Of course we all want to look our best, though. That kind of goes without saying. But that doesn't mean having to totally change everything about ourselves. People are going to such extremes, and they don't end up looking like themselves, when the real them is lovely.

I've done little things to change how I look. Like, I've got my nose pierced and I've had a few piercings in my ears, and I'd like a couple more. My nose was so painful to get done. My eyes were watering, and when I watched it back on camera it looked pretty gruesome, and I was surprised I went through with it, to be fair.

I haven't had any tattoos yet, although quite a lot of kids at my school had them. I think I would like to get a little one somewhere where no one can see it. I don't know what I want, so I won't get it done anytime soon, if I get it done at all. I'll see what happens. I might change my mind about it when I'm older anyway, so I won't rush into anything.

I don't mind the trend of having tons of tattoos, and it's totally up to people if they want to get them because it's their body, at the end of the day. I just don't think it's great when people get them just for the sake of it or to fit in with fashion, because trends come and go so quickly. A friend of my mum's has got a band of wire around her upper arm because it was a really cool thing to do in the '90s, but now she hates it and wishes she'd never done it.

I reckon you should wait and get something you love. I know you can get tattoos lasered off like Victoria Beckham and Rita Ora have, but that's supposed to be even more painful than getting the actual tattoo done. I don't fancy that at all. I'd rather not make the mistake in the first place.

It's awful when people get things spelt wrong. Or they get their boyfriend or girlfriend's name written on them, and then they split up. That is such a fail.

I saw this guy on a tattoo show who had a camel on his toe (get it?), and Jordan said he was going to get one. I was like, 'No you are not!' I guess it's quite funny to begin with, but the joke must wear a bit thin after a while. Especially when you're, like, eighty. Teardrops are horrible too. Imagine looking in the mirror every day and thinking, 'God, I look sad today.' 😢

I've had my teeth whitened, and that's a really quick and easy thing to do. I used to have really yellow teeth and someone commented on them online so I got self-conscious. I bought these whitening trays in America to start with, and then later on I got some proper ones made in the UK. They really work and it did give me a bit more confidence. Casey finds it hilarious when I've got the trays in because I can't talk properly. You may have seen it on one of my vlogs. I get a bit of a lisp and I can't pronounce certain words.

(Casey: 'You look and sound ridiculous. I can't believe you've left the house in them before.')

Five jobs I would be terrible at

1) Being a supermodel. Unless smaller models come into fashion.
2) Anything where I have to sit behind a desk.
3) A butcher, because the smell of fish and meat makes me gag.

(Mum: 'Saffron, you don't get fish in a butchers. You get it in a fishmongers.')

4) A mathematician, even if I was allowed to use the calculator on my phone.
5) A librarian. Can you imagine having to be quiet all the time?

Five jobs I would be good at

1) Primary school teacher. I'm really good with kids and I adore them.
2) Customer services. Although I would probably just talk to people all day.
3) Cabin crew. I love travelling so much, and it would be so cool.
4) Pop star. You've got to aim high!
5) Actress. I would love to be in a film one day.

August 5th

I've got a callback for the hair-curler job at the end of the month! I'm really, really excited. There are no guarantees, obviously, but it's so nice that they liked me. I'm going to do the best make-up ever. Beth offered to do it for me, but then she realized she's going be working that day so it's up to me to work my magic.

My make-up evolution!

Okay, so I've talked about how I first wore make-up when I was in Year Eight, but now I'm going to go into a bit more detail about my beauty regime in general.

When I first discovered foundation, I used to wear a really lightweight one and I built it up over time. But I definitely didn't always wear the right colour. I like to look tanned, so back in the day I thought the best way to get that look was to wear shades that were too dark for me. Cringe.

I also wouldn't blend them into my neck, so the darker colour would stop at my jawline and I'd look like I was wearing a creepy mask. When you put your make-up on, you kind of forget to turn to the side to see how it looks from another angle, and it's not until you go outside into daylight that you can <really> see it. If you don't realize, hopefully one of your mates will let you know if it's really bad.

These days, to avoid looking like I've drawn my face on with an orange crayon, I use a lighter foundation and then build up the colour with bronzer gradually. I'm using the Clinique Beyond Perfecting foundation at the moment, which I love. And primer-wise, I often use Benefit's The POREfessional and Too Faced's Hangover. I don't really suffer with dry skin, but I like it feeling smooth before I start building up a base, and they're both really good for that.

Bourjois foundations are brilliant as well, and my favourite concealer, which I use <every> single day, is The Collection Lasting Perfection. It's so cheap and it works so well. It's one of the things that YouTube made me buy!

I use a Beautyblender for everything, and that's changed my life. I used to buy fake ones, and then when I bought a real one I was like, 'What have I been doing?' It's <so> different. The fake ones seem to soak up all the foundation, but the real one smooths everything out.

I always set my face, and at the moment I'm using L'Oréal Infallible Fixing Mist or MAC Prep + Prime Fix+. When I've got my base in place, then it's time to start on the rest of my look.

Lipstick

I always wear lipstick, I don't feel like me without it. Some of the best ones I've ever tried are the liquid lipsticks by Anastasia Beverly Hills, which I buy whenever I'm in America. You can get them in the UK now, but sadly they're more expensive. They're unbelievable though.

I always put a liner on first and then put lipstick straight on with a wand because I find brushes fiddly. And I always ombré my lips. It's annoying for people when they ask me what colour I'm wearing, because I never just have one on. I prefer it to be lighter in the middle and darker on the outside because it makes your lips look fuller, and it's really pretty.

Matt lipsticks are really lovely, but the problem with them is that you can't reapply them. If you do, you get crumbly lips and it looks <awful>. If your lipstick starts to turn powdery, it's proper crisis time. You have to get to a bathroom as soon as you can and get it sorted out.

Eyebrows

In my opinion, eyebrows are one of the most important things when you're doing your make-up. They frame your face and if they look dodgy, it really shows.

My brows are microbladed now, but before I got that done I used to use a Sleek eyebrow kit. It isn't the most expensive one around, but it's really good. I was so nervous when I first had my microblading. The beautician who did them for me said I was the most nervous person she'd ever had to deal with. It's just so much easier now, though, because it means when I wake up my eyebrows aren't all over the place.

Microblading is honestly the only 'cosmetic' thing I've had done. People online have accused me of having Botox and cheek fillers, but I'm seventeen! I promise I've never had any of that stuff done. I know people are doing it younger and younger as a preventative thing, but there is no way a teenager needs their forehead frozen.

Skincare

Like most teenagers, I suffered from acne for a while. It kicked in when I was in Year Nine and my doctor told me to get E45 cream and use it as a face wash, and it really worked for me. It's really changed my skin and it's really affordable. I don't really need to use a moisturizer afterwards, and it gives me a really good base for my foundation. If I do ever feel like I need a bit of extra moisturizer, I'll use a Simple one.

Hair

My hair is wavy and disgustingly frizzy, but now I have extensions it's calmed down. I'm forever curling and straightening my hair, so it's not in the best condition, but having extensions kind of hides all of that.

My hair is naturally dark, dark brown, which everyone is always so surprised about. That's why my hair is so damaged, from being dyed. I've been having highlights since I was in Year Ten, so it's been through quite a lot!

I've always had long hair, but I've had those awful haircuts where you've gone in and asked for an inch off and they've snipped five off. That's the worst thing ever, because there's nothing you can do about it. It's so upsetting.

My go-to hairstyles

I love it when my hair is down, and then I put half of it up in a small bun at the back of my head. I also love a big messy bun. Fishtails are my saviour – I can't do braids, but I can do a fishtail in minutes, and they look super cute.

August 13th

My audition is so soon and I'm not going to lie, I've been practising some proper posing in front of the mirror. Obviously I'm already pretty good at selfies and being on camera, because I do that all the time, but this is a whole new level.

If I get the advert, it will be on TV screens across America, and also on billboards, which is <beyond> .

How to take the perfect selfie

Right guys, here's my guide to taking great selfies!

* Make sure the lighting is good. I always take my selfies with the phone flash on.
* Have a pop socket on your phone, because it makes it so

much easier to hold. Or use a selfie stick, although I find them fiddlier.

(Mum: 'Or use your mum's arm.')

I do like it when it looks like I'm taking the photo but actually my mum is, because the back camera on an iPhone is so much better than the front one.

- Find your angle! Practise taking selfies until you know which angle works best for you. Some people look great straight on, and some people suit it when their face is slightly to the side.
- Check your background! I'm quite bad for getting things in shot that shouldn't be there, so I would recommend that people look at what's in view before they take a picture. Casey left some empty bottles of beer in my room once. I got such a hammering online because people spotted them and accused me of drinking.

  I saw a hilarious photo of a woman who'd just done the marathon, and she was standing in her living room with her medal looking so happy. But when you looked behind her, she had big patio doors, and you could see her dog in the garden having a poo 💩.
- Mirror selfies are obviously brilliant if you love your outfit but your hair is a disaster. You can show off your swag but hide your face.
- Don't over-edit. I always use VSCO, which is my favourite

editing app. It's fine to put a filter on if the lighting isn't great, but don't make yourself look weird by blurring out your whole face.

Leonie and I went shopping today so I could get a new outfit for my audition. She has such amazing taste. She also wanted to get a new dress because she's got a date tonight.

We went to all the usual places we love, but she also took me to some vintage stores and also a flea market on Melrose. It was wall-to-wall hipsters and some of them were wearing the craziest outfits. I've always been a bit nervous about buying second-hand clothes. I don't know why, it's strange. We've got so many good vintage shops back in Brighton, but I always think that unless you know how to pull off that kind of look, you can end up looking like someone's nan.

Leonie can totally do vintage. She ended up getting this flowery maxi dress that she's going to wear with her biker boots. She tried the whole look on when she got home and I was like, 'Woah'. Honestly, if I'd tried that look I would <not> have got away with it.

I ended up buying a low V-neck white T-shirt with some really tiny silver stars around the top from this little boutique, and it's so nice on. I'm going to wear it with my new black skinny jeans from Urban Outfitters and some white Converse. I want to keep my look kind of simple.

My mum always bought me really cool clothes when I was growing up, but my own taste was not the best. I loved frilly dresses, and I would wear princess dresses out every single day like it was a totally normal thing to do. My favourite was Cinderella. It's a classic, isn't it? You can't go wrong. Jed and I wore matching outfits sometimes. I'd dress him up in wings and a dress, and push him around in his buggy.

(Casey: 'You do realize Jed's never going to speak to you again, don't you? Like, never?')

My mum wanted me to dress in trainers and leather jackets, so we had proper fashion wars. Looking back, I wish I'd listened to her because, oh my god, some of the photo evidence of my style choices is shocking.

Sometimes we'd compromise, and I'd wear a frilly dress and my mum would put a pair of Converse with it. But I would always fight to put fairy wings on, which would slightly ruin the overall look.

I feel like my taste has definitely got better as I've got older and I've developed my own style, but it's taken me a little while. I think you have to try a lot of clothes out to find out what works for you. Unfortunately, I didn't do that until I hit my teens.

As I've already mentioned, we're really honest as a family. Probably <too> honest, sometimes. My mum is the first person to tell me if something doesn't suit me. Even after I've bought something. Annoyingly, most of the time she's right.

Our daily routine generally goes like this:

I'll get something out of my wardrobe and put it on

She'll say, 'That isn't working, Saff.'

I'll realize she's right.

I'll ask her what I should wear and she'll say, 'Saffron, you're not seven years old! You can choose your own clothes.'

I'll be like, 'Well, I clearly can't.'

I'll be more confused than ever.

OR

I'll rebel and I won't change, and Mum will look at me and shake her head every time she sees me (maybe not every time, but quite a lot). Then I'll put the piece of clothing in the back of my wardrobe and never wear it again. But I still don't like to let her know she's won.

(Mum: 'Okay, and here's my side of the story! Saffron will come down in something new and I'll say, "Hmmmm, I'm not that keen on that", because I can't help but say what I think.

I do that to all my children and they do the same to me. Saffron isn't exactly shy about telling me when something doesn't look great on me either, to be fair!

'If an outfit is <really> bad, I will gently suggest that she could go and change it, especially if she's got a meeting. But I'm not bad all the time! I'll let her hang around the house in tracksuit bottoms and a stained hoodie, and not say anything. Most of the time.

'I always say to people that just because something is in fashion, it doesn't mean it's going to suit everyone, and I remind Saff of that all the time. You're better having your own style and wearing what suits you, rather than trying to fit in. She is really good at knowing what she does and doesn't like now, but we still all have the odd fashion fail.')

What I've learnt along the way (about fashion, not about, like, life)

Anything goes

These days, you can kind of wear anything you want. Double denim is perfectly acceptable, whereas if you wore a denim shirt and jeans a few years ago, people would have called you a double-denim disaster. Even proper granny-knitted jumpers have had their moment because hipsters love them, so don't be afraid to experiment.

Everyone should own a black leather jacket
My mum was right about leather jackets. You can literally wear one with anything, and it can dress an outfit up or down.

Backpacks are amazing
I saved up some money I'd earned from working and I treated myself to a Louis Vuitton backpack. I love it so much, I cried when I bought it. I use it all the time, so it was well worth it, even though it's one of the most expensive things I've ever bought. If you're going to use a bag every single day, I think it's worth investing in one that will last.

Take inspo, but don't copy
I don't have massive fashion icons, but there are people who I think look really cool, like Selena Gomez. She wears such cute outfits. Gigi Hadid looks good too, but I would never look like she does in her outfits because she's about 10 ft tall. I can take elements of what she wears, but I don't think skintight flares are for me. I also like boy fashion, like hoodies and baseball shirts, like Brooklyn Beckham and Jay-Z wear, so I'd consider them to be fashion inspirations too.

Keep everything!

My mum is always trying to throw my clothes away, but I'll hide things at the back of my wardrobe so she can't see them. You just never know when you might fall back in love with something. She threw away a tutu skirt I'd had for years and years recently, and I was so gutted. I really didn't need it anymore and I'll never wear it again, but I am quite sentimental about clothes. I've still got my first pink swimming costume, from when I was a baby, and I'll never get rid of that.

My mum is hardcore. She'll think nothing of giving stuff she thinks I won't need anymore to the charity shop. She's generally right about what I need to get rid of, which drives me mad. Sometimes I will try and argue my case, but she's pretty strict.

If it wasn't for my mum, I'd be a much worse hoarder than I am, so I worry about what will happen when I move out of home. I'll be one of those people you read about who can't leave their house because they've been trapped in by all their stuff.

Somehow a messy wardrobe works for me

Even though Mum stops me from being <too> messy, I still have a lot of clothes. I would love to have a massive walk-in closet where everything is organized by style and colour.

I want Hannah Montana's wardrobe. Hers was gigantic, and all she had to do was press her remote control and it would open up. All the drawers would slide out, so she could see exactly what she had. That is the life. Instead, I've got a floordrobe.

Sometimes a messy wardrobe <doesn't> work for me

My method of choosing what to wear is to pull out my entire wardrobe to find an outfit. There's no organization. It would change my life if someone put all my outfits together for me.

I used to quite like my school uniform, because at least I used to know what to wear five days a week. It was white and navy, and it was a real fashion thing to roll up your sleeves on your shirts. I'd add a belt around my skirt and wear long socks in the summer to make the whole look a bit cooler.

We were allowed to wear any kind of black shoes, boots or trainers, so I used to wear black, leather Converse and black, old-school Vans. I guess we were pretty lucky really. Some uniforms are really horrible.

The teachers were really laid-back about us wearing make-up and jewellery. Although, if anyone wore a nose ring you'd get chucked out of class and you'd have to hang out in an office with the teachers all day. Because of that, I waited until I left school to get mine done.

Things I would <never> wear

Real fur
I've worn fake fur and people have gone crazy at me. I once wore a fake-fur scarf and someone accused me of wearing a rabbit around my neck. As if!

Smart hats
I feel ridiculous in them. I'll wear caps and beanies, but trilbys just don't suit me.

Glove hats
I'm sorry, but those hats with gloves attached do not look good on me. The day I wear one of those is the day I've lost my mind.

Crazy earrings
I love big earrings, but proper comedy ones are a big no-no.

Boyfriend jeans
I love, love, love them on other people but because I'm small, they just don't suit me. Gutted.

Clashing prints
Some people can pull it off. But very few.

Christmas jumpers
That's such a lie. I wore one pretty much every day last Christmas.

August 28th

Today started off so well. I had my cute new top on, my make-up was on point and I was feeling <good>. I got an Uber to a rehearsal space downtown and I was pumped and ready to kill it at my audition. Then this happened:

I walk in. I see Anklet Girl from the last audition.

ME: *'Oh hi, you're back too! Good to see you.'*
HER: *'Hey, how's it going? Are you nervous?'*
ME: *'Oh yeah, super nervous. Have you done loads of these kinda things before?'*
HER: *'So many I've lost count. I haven't booked a job yet, but it's been okay because I do modelling as well as commercial work. I have to travel a lot, which I don't love, but it pays the bills.'*

(I am in no way surprised she's a model. She's properly gorgeous with glossy brown curls, massive green eyes and lips that would make Kylie Jenner feel jealous).

ME: *'You've got your anklet on again! It's so funny that we've got the same one. I want to go and get some as presents for my friends before I go home.'*
HER: *'I know. I literally never take mine off. It means the world*

to me because my boyfriend Ryan gave it to me for our one-year anniversary at the end of last month.'

(I swallow. <Hard>.

It can't be.

It <can't> be.)

Me: *'Cool.'*

(Ask her. Don't worry, it won't be the same one. It can't be the same one.)

Me: *'What does Ryan do?'*

(She doesn't need to answer. Her phone rings and a photo of a guy flashes up. I recognize the sun-kissed hair. I know those piercing blue eyes. And there is no mistaking the mouth that's been telling me lie after lie for the last seven months.

There's silence. She looks at me in horror and she knows. Neither of us needs to say anything because my expression is clearly saying it all. We both look down at our anklets and then at each other.)

Me: *'Oh my god, I'm so sorry. I didn't know he had a girlfriend.'*

(She looks down.)

Her: *'How long?'*

Me: *'We met in January. If I'd known . . .'*

(My voice trails off. Nothing I can say right now will help the situation.

She looks up at me, and I can see that I'm not the only one with tears in my eyes.)

Her: *'It's not your fault. I had a feeling. It's not the first time he's cheated on me. I found out he was seeing someone else a couple of months after we got together, but he swore it was nothing. I should have dumped him there and then, but he promised me it would never happen again.'*

(Her tears start falling harder, and I lean forward to give her a hug.)

Her: *'I just feel like such an idiot. He convinced me to move in with him six months ago, and I knew it was a bad idea. I should have listened to my gut.'*

(I went to his place for dinner in June. Oh my god, have I been to <their> apartment? There definitely wasn't any girls' stuff around. I even checked the bathroom cabinet (don't judge me, everyone does it).)

Me: *'Erm, I hate to ask this but I'm so confused. Is your apartment all white, with loads of glass and an open-plan kitchen and living-room area?'*

(She shakes her head and lets out a little laugh.)

Her: *'Oh god, he's such an idiot. That's his booker's apartment. He was housesitting for him for a week and he obviously thought it would be a great opportunity to impress you.'*

My mind starts whirring. It all makes so much sense. No wonder Ryan didn't invite me round to 'his' place for so long. And no wonder he always insisted on meeting at my house, or acted shady when we were out. The few times we had gone out together, his poor girlfriend was probably away modelling, which meant there wasn't much chance of him getting caught out.

I feel like I'm going to be sick. There is no way I can stay for the audition. My face is all red and puffy, and I'm just not going to be able to put on a happy face for the camera. All I want to do is go home, get into bed, phone my mum and cry some more.

I give Anklet Girl a long, apologetic hug and then I bolt out and make a run for the nearest taxi. I have no idea if she's going to stay and see the audition through, but I wish her luck as I leave. With <everything>.

CHAPTER 9

September

September 6th

It's been over a week since I found out Ryan was a cheating, stupid, deceitful, annoying, heartbreaking piece of . . . The following things have got me through:

My mum.
Leonie and Beth.
Ice cream.
More ice cream.
Tissues.
TopShop.

I was on the phone to Mum for two hours last night, and she got really upset, which I felt terrible about. She hates it when I'm sad and she said she felt useless being so far away. But she helped me masses.

She reminded me of how bad I felt when I split up with my ex, and that I moved on and I got over him. And she's right. It always feels like the end of the world when you first break up with someone, and you think you're never going to feel 'normal' again. And then one day you realize you do. You get to the end of the day and you suddenly think, 'I haven't thought about them today.' When you do that, you know it's only a matter of time before you're totally moving on.

Mum also pointed out what a lucky escape I'd had. I guess because I didn't see Ryan every day, I didn't fall for him as much as I would have done if we'd been by each other's sides 24/7.

I'm really the one who's come out of this the best. My heart may be hurting and I'm gutted he let me down, but at least I'm not a massive cheater. It sucks to be him.

Ryan has tried to phone me, like, fifty times, but I refuse to answer. I am not going to make things easy for him. I want him to feel horrible for what he's done. He's left me so many messages, telling me he wants to explain. Explain what? That's he's basically a really terrible person?

None of his voicemails actually make any sense. He's just

rambling and saying sorry loads of times. <What>.< Ever>. You can take your sorry, and your (annoyingly) very pretty eyes, and do one. I hope Anklet Girl has dumped you and you're alone. Possibly forever.

Leonie and Beth have been amazing. They've been so supportive and sweet. Leonie made me a 'break-up dinner', and she basically tried to recreate Nando's chicken for me. How sweet is that? She did a really good job. Then we watched some romantic movies, and she told me over and over again how much of an idiot Ryan was. Without using the words 'I told you so', even though, to be fair, she basically did.

It's funny how you sometimes know that people are right, but you kind of block out what they're saying because you want to believe something else (wow, that is <deep>). My instincts told me that there was something not right about Ryan. For a start, he wore sunglasses inside, even when it was dark. That alone should have been a massive warning sign.

I also realized that, looking back, I didn't laugh a lot with him, and that is so important when you're with someone. I always thought he thought he was a little bit better than me, and like he was doing me a favour by actually ever seeing me. What is that?

I managed to push all my worries about him to the back of my mind because I wanted it to work out so badly. I guess he was also a bit of a comfort blanket (I don't mean like he *was big and fluffy, because he really wasn't), because I was so far from home and feeling a bit lonely. Now I realize the way he acted probably made me feel lonelier, if anything.*

I've vlogged about the break-up a few times and my viewers have been unbelievable. The support has been beyond. Everyone has been so kind, and I'm actually so relieved Ryan didn't ever appear in any of my vlogs, because I can't imagine how much hassle he would have got. Whenever anything goes wrong, my crew are right on my side, and I wouldn't want them wasting their time or energy on him.

Where would we be without friends? Who would put on disgusting homemade face packs with us, and laugh about ridiculous things we've done?

I've had a lot of the same friends for a long time, and they literally mean everything to me. But I wasn't the girl at school who had a million mates and was always rushing around trying to keep up with everyone. I prefer having a small group who are really close. Some of my friends at school had massive extended squads, but that wasn't for me. I had to give up going to a lot of the parties and hanging out after school for the band, and also when I started YouTube.

I've never been a people pleaser and I've never wanted to be liked just for the sake of being popular. I didn't ever have a problem with anyone and I got on with everyone, so it wasn't like I was an outcast or anything. But I didn't feel like I had to be queen bee 🐝.

I've got so many friends that I've met via YouTube now, which is so nice, because we've got so much in common. My old friends often ask me how YouTube is going and it's great to be able to talk to them about it, but I guess the other YouTubers and I can really relate to each other. We've been through a lot of the same stuff and we've had similar things happen to us. They've had to deal with people giving them a hard time sometimes, and also with making sacrifices for work, which can prove tricky sometimes.

I'm definitely more careful about who I let into my life these days, big time. People always ask me if doing YouTube can be lonely, and being totally honest? It can be, sometimes. You have to be wary of who you're opening up to. You can do one tiny thing wrong on social media, and it will completely mess you up. I've seen it happen to people, and it's scary. It only takes one person to try and bring you down, and that could be it. It's a horrible thing to think about that, but I guess I do have to protect myself.

You can have millions of friends online and sometimes you just want to hang out with <one> person, and my friends are often busy at the opposite times to me. I'm mainly free during the week when my friends are working, or they're at college, and that can be tough. Then, when they want to hang out at weekends, I'll be at an event or filming, and that's frustrating at times.

We all have those moments where we want to be with a really good friend to talk about everything and nothing. My online friends are literally incredible, but sometimes I crave face-to-face conversations and the chance to be like a total kid again.

I met a really cool girl once, and we were really similar and we had a real laugh together. We started hanging out and we had so much in common. She seemed to like all the same things I liked and she even started dressing more like me. I was really flattered and thought it was cool that we were quite twinny. I imagined us being friends for years and sharing loads of cool experiences.

In fact, this is what actually happened. The girl, who I will not name, started dressing even <more> like me, to the point where she'd turn up to meet me in the same <actual> clothes that I had. She also started doing her hair and make-up like mine. It all started to feel a bit weird. We were still getting on really well, so I let it slide and tried not to read too much into it.

A few weeks later, I noticed that her attitude towards me changed. She became a bit distant and started to put me down. I could tell something wasn't right. Then she cut contact with me. I was, like, so confused.

A few days after that, I noticed on YouTube that she'd started her own channel and I felt like she was basically copying my life, my words and my ideas. I felt so let down. It really stung. If she'd asked me, I would have been really happy to help her out so she could find her own 'thing'. Instead, it felt like she wanted to basically use my style to become successful.

I love other YouTubers and I honestly don't feel like I'm competing with any of them, and it would have been the same with her. She just went about things in such a weird way. I haven't heard from her since and that makes me feel a bit gutted. It was a harsh but good lesson for me. She did me a favour, because she showed me what I needed to look out for, and helped me realize that not everyone who comes into my life is going to be there for the right reasons.

Everyone goes through tricky times with friends sometimes, and that situation was pretty extreme. If ever I have an issue with one of my friends or they have an issue with me, we'll just be upfront about it. It's the only way to resolve things. Sticking your head in the sand doesn't work, because things still need to be dealt with. Deal and move on and your friendship will be stronger for it (unless they try to steal your life, which is <not> okay).

I think if you ever argue with your friends, it should always be the person who's in the wrong who apologizes. But quite often both people will think they're in the right, so that's hard! I can't remember the last time I fell out with any of my friends, because we literally love each other. If it ever did happen, I would like to think I'd be big enough to make the first move. Life's too short for fallouts.

Friendship goals

1) Loyalty. That's my number-one thing. Friends always have to have your back.
2) Honesty. I'm a very truthful friend, and I expect other people to be too.
3) Laughter. I love someone who makes me laugh. It shows how similar you are.
4) Shopping. It's honestly important that someone likes shopping as much as I do!
5) Understanding. Sometimes I am really busy with work, and my friends are really cool if I can't see them for a little while. They get it.

September 17th

I thought I saw Ryan today. I didn't. But the fact I thought I did, and so sort of did, made me feel funny. I actually didn't feel as sick as I thought I would. I think I must be getting over him. I really hope Anklet Girl is okay. It must have been so much worse for her. The poor girl shared her whole life with him.

I doubt it will be hard for her to meet someone else. I bet she can't walk to the end of her road without being asked out. But it's not really about that, is it? Just because you're beautiful, it doesn't mean your heart doesn't break as hard or that you hurt less. I'm sending her loads of 'feel better soon' vibes.

September 27th

You generally do two things when you go through a break-up. You either comfort-eat, or you decide to make yourself feel better by eating really healthily and exercising. Or, if you're me, you do both.

I've eaten so much Ben & Jerry's, there's a danger of me turning into one of those chocolate fish (or 'phish', as they call them), so it's time to crack out the Lycra and get back to the gym.

Leonie isn't a big gym-lover but Beth is going to come with me. She's also going to see if she can book us into a class at Soul Cycle. It's really hard to get in there, but she's got connections and I love the idea of finding myself sweating like mad sat on a bike next to Brooklyn Beckham.

Oh dear. I totally haven't thought that through properly, have I?

I have a kind of love/hate relationship with the gym. I find it really boring unless I do classes like Body Attack, Body Pump and Body Combat. At least with them, it's like I'm forced into exercising, because once I'm in a class I have to do it. You can't really do a runner halfway through without everyone seeing.

I've got a personal trainer I see sometimes, and he's really good at making me do things I don't like. Usually while I moan a lot.

One January, I promised myself I was going to start going to the gym three or four times a week. I bought some really nice new gym gear and I was so ready. I was going to look so cool. And I wasn't going to hang out by the water cooler in full make-up like I had done before. I was going to <work it>.

I went into the main gym, and I decided this was going to be the time when I fell in love with running. So I got on a treadmill, with my new Lycra glistening under the bright gym lights, and I sped it up. You know that saying, 'Don't try and run before you can walk?' That wasn't me that day. I ramped up the speed and threw myself into it. My iPhone was turned up, I was focused and I was imagining myself running marathons without breaking a sweat in the very near future.

Then my legs started to slow down, like I had no control over them. I think they'd got a bit tired, even though my brain was still pumped, and all of a sudden I realized that the treadmill was going a lot faster than my legs could. I tried to pick up the pace but it was no good, and I soon found myself sliding off the end of it, still clinging onto the rails.

The other thing that's so bad is when I get wind in the classes. I'll always look at my mum, and she'll know, and I can't control it. People always think it's her, because I keep a serious face on, but she giggles when she knows I've farted. I also have to be careful I don't do star jumps when I've got a full bladder either, otherwise I want to wee. How uncool would it be if you did a wee in a class? No one at my gym is going to want to be in classes with me after that.

The best thing about the gym for me is the clothes. Everything has to be matching, and I usually wear tight yoga shorts or leggings with a crop top and a baggy top over the top.

I love the look of gym clothes. Sometimes that alone will make me want to go and work out. I don't wear a lot of make-up to the gym, like I used to, but I will admit to a little bit of foundation, some mascara and filling in my eyebrows. I try not to go too far, but I think it's unfair on other people if I don't wear a little bit. People always comment on my vlog, going, 'Why is she wearing make-up to the gym?' but it's more for other people's benefit 😂.

If I've got a tan I don't bother, but if I haven't, I look a bit unwell. Also, I know loads of people there, so I've got to look half-decent!

I watch a lot of fitness YouTubers, and I follow a lot of super-fit and healthy pages on Instagram. Going to the gym isn't just about weight loss. For me, it's about feeling fit and well. I sit on my backside a lot when I'm making videos and editing, and because I'm so short of time, I'll end up getting a bus into a town instead of walking. I love the buzz I get after exercising. I just don't always enjoy every minute of it.

I've got better with my gym-going. I totally used to be that girl who stood around with a full face of make-up on, checking out the boys, but now when I see other girls do that I think, 'WTF?' I love watching the Top 40 on the TVs in the gym, because that makes me forget I'm exercising. I don't get a lot of time to watch TV at home, so it's a nice time to get updated. And if I see Beyoncé swinging around a pole, looking amazing, that makes me work harder. In my head, it's only a matter of time before I look like her.

I make playlists for the iPhone and the person who makes me really go for it is Flo Rida, and my current favourite album is Ed Sheeran's *Multiply*. I don't have to listen to fast music in the gym to pump me up. I'm quite happy for the music to be mid-tempo.

I would love to do a marathon, but I can't see it happening. I did a Warrior Run with my family, which was hilarious. It was a seven-mile obstacle course. It kicked off with us running down a ditch into some water, and it practically covered my entire head. I was soaked.

I fell over about 100 times, but my mum had the biggest fail when she went down an inflatable slide into some muddy water. This man crashed into her and she went right underneath, so her head and everything were covered. She was screaming like mad, and I filmed it. It's one of my favourite videos ever. The mud stank, and instead of helping her, we were all laughing while she disappeared into this mud like it was quicksand. I'm not the fittest person in the world, but I loved it and I gave it all I've got. I'll definitely do it again.

I often get bored when I'm running in the gym, so I start thinking about totally weird things. Today I started thinking about what would happen if you didn't have any thumbs.

Would you still be able to do push-ups?

How could you hold cutlery?

What about writing? You wouldn't be able to hold a pen!

Typing would be so much slower.

Imagine trying to squeeze out toothpaste? It would go everywhere.

You'd have to get someone to open packets of sweets and crisps for you. And what if no one was around? I feel panicked just thinking about it.

I wouldn't be able to throw balls for Bella. She's usually too lazy to go and fetch them but I'd like to have the option just in case.

I always use my thumb to turn over the TV with the remote – disaster!

It would be impossible to thumb wrestle (I've actually never done that in my life).

I'd have to get people to turn door handles for me. What if I got stuck in the bathroom with nothing to do? It would be so boring.

And counting to five on one hand would be impossible.

How would you do a thumbs-up? You couldn't. End of.

And scariest of all, how would you text?!

I now have a newfound appreciation for my thumbs. They're pretty amazing.

CHAPTER 10

October

October 9th

I am loving the gym! Seriously, it's giving me loads of much-needed energy and focus right now. Ryan who?

I'm also so excited about Christmas. I've been making plans already, because I'll be back home soon and there's lots to organize.

This month is going to be all about vlogging and videos, and I'm so excited for that. But I just know that by the end of it, I'll be so close to seeing my family again. I really hope Bella isn't missing me too much. I miss ruffling her crazy nana hair.

October 17th

I am <so> proud of Leonie. She's been working really hard lately, and it seems like it's all about to pay off. She got a call today from a big fashion company who want to talk to her about designing a range for them. She literally deserves it so much.

We did such a cool video yesterday, where we told each other facts about ourselves and we had to say whether we thought they were true or false. We already know so much about each other, but there's also tons we don't know. That's the fun thing about making new friends. You have so much to discover about them.

I guessed right that Leonie used to do ballet when she was younger, and that she was the head cheerleader at her school. The second one was really obvious because she would totally have been the popular girl at school (but not in, like, a mean-girl way). She's effortlessly cool. I swear, everything she puts on looks good. She can wear jeans and a plain white T-shirt, but then she'll accessorize so well, it will still look like she planned her outfit out for days.

Leonie guessed right that I won a singing competition when I was ten. But she also thought I was telling the truth when I said I was the British tap-dancing champion at fourteen.

Cringe! I'm hoping she was joking about that because, if not, I'm giving off some seriously uncool vibes. (Having said that, I actually really enjoyed tap-dancing.)

October 24th

Leonie's done it! She's signed a deal to create a capsule range for one of the biggest high-street stores in the US! She is <so> clever, and I'm so proud of her. We celebrated by drinking milkshakes and eating a lot of cake at our favourite diner.

Beth came along too, and the three of us laughed so much, the waitress asked if we were okay because we all had thick lines of mascara and eyeliner running down our faces. I am beyond lucky I found those girls. I genuinely think we'll be friends forever.

October is definitely one of my favourite months. I start planning my autumn videos in August, and it's such a big thing on YouTube. Everything changes, because the clocks go back. I buy double the number of candles because I'll have them on non-stop. I always stock up in Bath and Body Works if I'm in America, because they do the best ones.

If you'd asked me about my favourite time of year two years ago, I would always have said summer, but now the run-up to Christmas is totally my favourite. I literally love autumn so much. Which, incidentally, is my middle name.

Five names I wish I'd been called

1) Sapphire (it's such a dramatic name, it's cool if you rock it out)
2) Kendall
3) Edie
4) Ava
5) Brooklyn (who cares if it's not a girl's name?).

Weird fact: When I used to play Mums and Dads with my friends at school, I always used to pretend that my child was called Angelica because I loved *Rugrats*. I don't think it's a name I'll be using, though.

Autumn is great because it's so nice cuddling up and watching movies, or going to the cinema. I spend so much money on going to the cinema with my friends. I love it. I would go literally every day if I had time.

Going to the cinema feels like a real treat, and it's such a cold weather thing to do. I always get chocolate raisins to eat while I watch the film. I love them so much, sometimes I'll go to the cinema just so I can have them. I also love Mars and Boost minis. In fact, I love all mini-chocolates. I can't eat a whole bar of chocolate in one go, because it feels like too much. But if they're broken down like that, it's so much easier to eat <tons> without noticing. It's bad, but also really, really good.

I totally shamed myself in my local cinema when I went to meet a load of friends recently. I was late (as per usual) and, as I ran down the stairs into the cinema, I tripped over and face-planted on the floor. I'm not exaggerating when I say that everyone turned around and laughed at me. It really wasn't my fault. It was so sad. They turn the lights off <way> too early in my opinion.

Another good thing about this time of year is that I can go out and get a new winter coat. I am a bit obsessed with coats, generally. I prefer dressing for winter because you can chuck on a jumper and jeans, and it's so much easier. I love buying woolly hats, and shopping for gloves and scarves. And I can finally wear boots again! I can also start layering my clothes, and the colours are so lovely.

Dressing for summer is hard, especially because, as you know, I <don't> like my feet, so wearing flip-flops is a nightmare. I also like winter because you can wear jeans. Everyone thinks leggings are so much more comfortable than jeans, but I disagree.

My nan finds my jeans ridiculous, because she doesn't understand why they're all ripped. The other day she asked me if I got a discount because there was so much of them missing. Really funny, Nan!

October 31st

There are so many things I love about the UK but – and don't kill me for saying this – America is <so> much better at doing Halloween. They take it really seriously (if you can take Halloween seriously), and it's almost as big as Christmas over here. The shops are full of costumes and decorations and sweets, and the kids get so much candy they don't know what to do with it. When I was a kid, we'd think we were really lucky if one house out of twenty answered the door, let alone gave us sweets!

The best thing was that my mum always used to buy sweets just in case loads of trick or treaters came round, and they never did, so my brothers and I got to eat it all the following day.

Leonie has gone to see her family, but Beth is taking me to a party that's doubling up as a wrap party for the zombie film she's been working on, and I can't wait.

I've been agonizing over what to dress up as for weeks, and it's hard because you can be literally anything. You don't even have to be scary. Some people go out dressed as celebrities or superheroes. It's more like a massive fancy-dress party than about being really frightening.

The outfit I've chosen is – drum roll – Dorothy from The Wizard of Oz. *I haven't dressed up like her since I was a kid, so I thought it would be funny. Beth is going to do some scary make-up on one side of my face so it looks like it's melting (cool, huh?). I've even got a little stuffed dog to carry around with me!*

Halloween is so much fun, and I go to the same Fright Night event every year, which is petrifying but brilliant. I go with my friends, and I always vlog it. Thorpe Park do an amazing Fright Night too, so I go there whenever I can.

My mum always decorates our house so amazingly. We have cobwebs everywhere, and loads of decorations. I usually dress up as a distressed schoolgirl, and rip up my old uniforms

and cover myself in fake blood. It's simple but effective!

We did the best prank on my dad last year, when we decided to fill his beloved car with 300 pumpkins. We went to Asda and bought them and we transported them back to my house to put in Mum's car. We had to get them out of Mum's car into my dad's, and we used a great technique, which involved throwing them at the nearest person and hoping they didn't drop them. At one point we decided to open the back of Mum's car to get more out, and they all fell out and started rolling around. It was so annoying.

When we knew Dad was coming back, we all hid behind a wall and jumped out, and I filmed the whole thing. His reaction was absolutely brilliant. He flipped. All he was worried about was the suspension on his car, and the fact he was supposed to be at a meeting in fifteen minutes' time. There wasn't much chance of him driving the car anywhere.

Dad opened the door and loads of pumpkins came tumbling out. One fell right on his leg, which he was not happy about. I thought it was so funny, but it was so annoying taking the pumpkins out of the car afterwards. We didn't want to throw them away, so we left them outside the house and put up signs saying, 'Please take as many as you want.'

It was two days before Halloween, so they went really quickly. It was like we did a pumpkin car-boot sale. Except we didn't actually earn any money from it.

CHAPTER 11
November

November 1st

Oh my god, the party was, like, so fun. Beth did my make-up so amazingly, I even scared myself when I looked in the mirror. The party was in a big warehouse downtown, and I felt a bit strange on the journey there. I've been in LA for over ten months now and, while I am looking forward to going home next month, I'll be sad to leave here.

It's been such an experience, but I don't think I've ever properly settled. If you get what I mean? I feel like I've been on a massive long holiday. The people are super friendly and the restaurants are amazing. Did I tell you that you get free refills on soft drinks most places you go? I've only ever really experienced that in Nando's back home, so my Diet Coke obsession has been a bit out of control over here.

I loved seeing the bright lights of LA whizzing past as our Uber zoomed down the wide roads. It really is exactly what you expect it to be. There are billboards everywhere and flashing neon signs, and everyone who's come out here searching for fame dreams of seeing their name and face on one of them.

I spend my days passing people in the streets and thinking, 'I know you from somewhere', and everyone you meet is hoping you may be able to do something for them. I've lost count of the total strangers who have asked if they can appear in one of my vlogs or videos when they find out how many subscribers I've got.

Leonie and I hiked up to the Hollywood sign last month (it's, like, one of the things you have to do when you come to LA – it would be strange if you didn't), and obviously I did vlog it (even though at some points I was so breathless I could hardly speak).

At one point, I looked at my camera screen and realized I could see loads of people behind me. When I turned around, a crowd had gathered, and they were all trying to get into the back of my shot! They probably didn't even know who I was or what I was filming for, but I think people see an opportunity every time they see a camera.

It's a strange thing, because I totally get why people want to be famous and have all this success. But I also feel like my life would still be so cool even if I didn't ever become a big movie star or whatever. I don't feel like my whole life depends on it. Would I like Katy Perry's career, Jessie J's voice and to be competing with Hailee Steinfeld for acting roles? Sure. Would I feel like I'd failed if I didn't do all those things? No way. And it's funny how sometimes things fall into your lap when you're not actually looking for them.

So, the party was super cool and some of the zombies were <hot>. They were covered in blood and stuff, and one of them had a fake eye dangling on his cheek, but he totally still had 'something'. The warehouse had been decked out to look like an underground bunker, and it was really dark and eerie. Some of the actors from the film were in disguise, and they would jump out at you when you were least expecting it. I screamed so loudly at one point, a woman standing near me dropped her drink.

I was expecting most of the people there to think they were a bit too cool to speak to me, but everyone was, like, <so> friendly. Beth knew so many people, so we were kind of going from one group to another, chatting, and loads of them were like, 'We love your accent.' I get that a lot out here.

Then the funniest thing happened completely out of the blue. I mean it was, like, <so> unexpected. I got offered my first movie role! Yes, you did read that right. A MOVIE ROLE.

Basically, Beth introduced me to Martin, the director of the movie, which is called, wait for it – Beware! Zombies Want to Eat You *– and she mentioned that I'd love to do some acting (I don't think he was that surprised – Beth and Leonie are probably the only people in Hollywood who don't).*

He said to me, 'We're actually looking for a British girl to star in the sequel. It's only a small role, and you get killed in the opening credits, but we've all got to start somewhere!'

So there you have it. I officially have a role as 'British girl who gets killed really quickly' in Beware! Zombies Want to Eat You 2.

I cannot <wait> to tell Jed. He will be so jealous.

November 5th

It feels strangely quiet over here tonight. The US don't celebrate Bonfire Night because, obviously. it's all to do with Guy Fawkes trying to blow up the Houses of Parliament, like, <years> ago, and the Americans aren't fussed about it (do you feel like this is a really good history lesson? I feel quite proud of myself).

I feel sad that I won't be 'oohing' and 'ahhhhing' at Catherine wheels this year. I might have to buy myself some indoor sparklers from the local store and have a very, very small fireworks celebration on my own, in my room.

We have got Thanksgiving later this month, which is a massive celebration that happens all across America. Leonie is so excited about it. I didn't really understand it, so I Googled it to find out what it was all about and it said this:

> *Thanksgiving, or Thanksgiving Day, is a public holiday celebrated on the fourth Thursday of November in the United States. It originated as a harvest festival.*

Thanksgiving has been celebrated nationally on and off since 1789, after a proclamation by George Washington. It has been celebrated as a federal holiday every year since 1863.

It sounds pretty complicated, but I think it basically means everyone gets together and has a really good time and says thank you for all the nice things they have. Not, like, trainers and computers and things, but family and friends and food.

I also found out during my Google research that 46 million turkeys are eaten across the US over the weekend. <46 million>? 

It's good for me, because I like turkey. Not as much as chicken, but if I put enough sauce on it, I really can't tell the difference.

★ ★ ★

In honour of the amazing turkey fact above, here are some random facts about me (you won't know how you lived without them for so long)

* My two favourite traits in people are honesty and loyalty.
* I'm addicted to chewing gum.
* I hate seafood.

* My biggest fears are death and losing my loved ones.
* When I was born, I had my umbilical cord wrapped around my neck, so I stopped breathing for a few seconds.
* My favourite flowers are roses.
* I'm extremely messy.
* Seeing the Northern Lights and hiking up to the Hollywood sign were on my bucket list, and I've done them both now. They were absolutely amazing experiences.
* I have size six and a half feet.
* I've had grommets six times and thirteen operations on my ears.

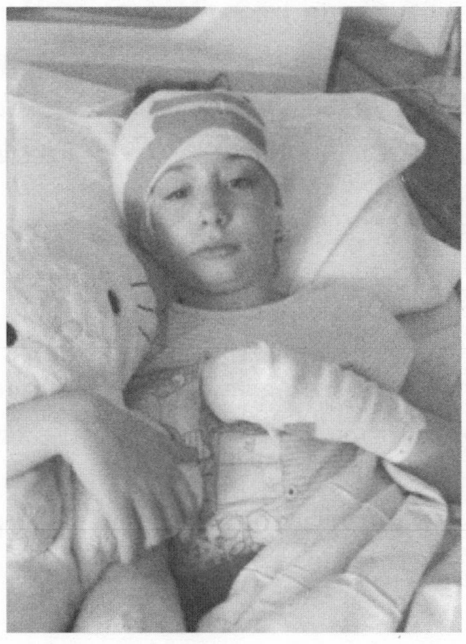

It was awful, but I was so well looked after and I even got to drive a toy motorbike down the hallway of the hospital, which was a big life highlight.

★ The first phone I ever had was a pink slide-up phone, and I loved it. It honestly changed my life.

★ One of my favourite quotes is: 'And if you're ever feeling lonely, just look at the moon. Someone, somewhere is looking right at it too.'

★ The most awkward conversation I've ever had was when I told my mum I started my periods. I was so embarrassed. She told my dad, and then my older brother found out. I was so mortified, and I didn't think I could face them.

★ My perfect party would involve all of my family and friends together, lots of good food, boys, getting really dressed up and good music. So basically, it would probably be like most people's perfect party.

★ My perfect night in would be all about pampering, which I love. I'd put on face masks and watch *Vampire Diaries*, because I never get bored of it.

★ The most random thing that's ever happened to me was when I was in Amsterdam. Casey and I went to the spa and when we climbed into the hot tub, there was another guy already in there. One of his mates came in and said, 'Alright, Shawn?' <That's> when we realized it was Shawn Mendes. #oblivious

* The things that are always in my bag are: gum, my phone charger, my purse, sunglasses, deodorant, Jimmy Choo perfume and a bottle of water. There are always old receipts (probably with chewing gum inside), loose change and broken nails at the bottom of my bag.
* My dream dinner-party guests would be Zac Efron, Melissa McCarthy, Kevin Hart, James Corden, Dwayne Johnson, Selena Gomez, the Beckhams, Jessie J and Ed Sheeran. I wouldn't cook though. I'd order in.
* I hate having a cold nose. When I used to walk to high school with my friends in the winter, from Year Seven to Year Eleven, I was always freezing. We always had those heated hand warmers and I had to hold it to my nose all the time. It was always the part of me that got coldest and I hated it. I want to invent a transparent nose warmer that sticks to your nose and keeps it really warm, but which no one will be able to see. That would honestly change my life.
* The thing I wish I'd invented is Google, Facebook or anything by Apple, because I'd be a millionaire now.
* If I could swap lives with anyone for the day, I'd become Brooklyn Beckham. I'd make 'him' follow all my social media accounts, and I'd put pictures of myself up everywhere, so he would have no choice but to fall in love with me. Joking aside, I would like to be a boy for a day to see what it's like to be inside their heads. What would I think about? Probably

computer games and what was for dinner. I'd also like to be Jessie J, because I'm in love with her voice. Or Selena Gomez, to see what it's like to live her amazing life.

* My favourite film is *The Last Song.* Miley Cyrus is in it and it's the saddest, most amazing movie ever. I've seen it twenty-two times, and I would watch it more but I've promised my friend Georgia that I'll only ever watch it with her. My ex was always desperate to watch it with me, but I refused because I couldn't break my promise. I love *The Amazing Spider-Man* too. I love watching action movies and it's the best one. It's so cool. Also, *Diary of a Wimpy Kid* and *Dork Diaries* are still some of my favourite books. They're so cute.
* My favourite band growing up was JLS, and I always listened to Destiny's Child and En Vogue. I definitely prefer Destiny's Child to Beyoncé's solo stuff. They were so good together.
* I don't watch a lot of TV, but *I'm a Celebrity . . .* is my favourite show by far when I do. And *Love Island* is addictive.
* I was in one of Alex Aiono's videos one time. I was telling my friend how much I loved him one night, and the following morning when I woke up his manager had messaged me to tell me that Alex would love to me to be in his video. How weird is that?

But, oh my god! I was BUSY! I had a work thing booked

in that I couldn't change, which was so gutting. In the end I managed to race over in the evening, so I still got to be in the video, and he was such a nice guy.

Why I love Bonfire Night

Generally on Bonfire Night, I'll spend an hour trying to decide which coat I want to wear, wrap fifty scarves around my neck and then head out to watch fireworks with my family. We usually go somewhere around Brighton, and I love it.

It's not just about the fireworks, although they're very cool. It's more about how snug and cute it is. We always have hot chocolate and we'll go for dinner either before or afterwards. 🔥🔥🔥🔥🔥🔥🔥🔥🔥🔥🔥🔥🔥🔥🔥🔥🔥🔥🔥🔥🔥

The nine things I'd save first if my house was on fire

1) Bella. She'd be the first thing I'd grab if she hadn't got out on her own.
2) My laptop. It's my life. I'd be devastated if I lost it.
3) My camera and my SD cards, because I wouldn't want to lose all my old footage.
4) My phone. For obvious reasons.
5) My passport, so I can go on a nice holiday once the insurance payout comes through.
6) Old photos, because they're not on my phone.

7) My dressing gown, so I wouldn't have to stand around in the street in my pyjamas.
8) My make-up bag. I would be so sad if I lost all of my favourite cosmetics.
9) My Tiffany necklace, because it means a lot to me.

November 30th

You won't believe who I saw today. Don't worry, it's not Ryan, but it's pretty close. Yes, you guessed it, I saw Anklet Girl. I was just coming out of the gym when I spotted my dream workout look, and she was inside of it. I literally gasped when I saw her, because I felt super awkward, but she ran over and gave me a massive hug.

Her: *'How are you? I've been meaning to get in touch with you but I didn't have your details, and I thought it might be a bit public over Twitter or Instagram . . .'*
Me: *'I'm doing really well. But how are you? I've been thinking about you.'*
Her: *'You know, I'm okay. Ryan and I broke up, of course, and he moved out a couple of weeks after I last saw you. He*

was "really, really sorry", but I'd heard it all before. You did me such a massive favour. If I hadn't bumped into you that time, I would never have known what he was up to. He's so stupid. He had two great girls and he lost them both. I heard he's seeing some other chick, but how long until he cheats on her too? Once a cheater, always a cheater. And anyway, I've met someone new. It's early days, but he's cool. How about you?'

Me: *'I'm still single. But do you know what? That suits me right now. I've been messaging a few guys from back home, and I'm meeting up with one next week. But if there's one thing that being in LA has taught me, it's that I'm pretty good at being on my own. It would be nice to meet someone, but I've got so much going on, a guy would be the icing on the cake, rather than the cake itself.'*

As I said those words, I realized I truly believed them. When I moved out here, I was still heartbroken from my ex. Then Ryan stitched me up and I thought I was destined to meet losers. But now I know when I meet someone new, it will be on my terms because I deserve the <best>.

Anklet Girl, who I now know is called River (of course she is, she's cool <as well> as beautiful!), skipped her yoga class and we went for a long lunch together. It turns out that, despite her tear-stained face, she got the hair-curling gig, and I'm *genuinely happy for her. She's going to be on one of those massive billboards on Hollywood Boulevard and she's freaking out. I just can't wait for Ryan to see it.*

River and I are going to do a video together tomorrow. Ryan is going to hate it *. And once that's done, I'm done with being in the least bit bothered about Ryan. He's in my past, and my future is far more important.*

★ ★ ★

CHAPTER 12

December

December 3rd

I'm flying home soon. I can't quite believe it. I'll be back in America next March to film my zombie role, but other than that it's bye-bye LA for now.

I hope I can fit all my new clothes into my suitcase. It's a genuine worry. I need my mum to go through them all and be ruthless, but if it gets too bad, I'll have to donate some things to Beth and Leonie.

We're going for a goodbye dinner tomorrow and I just know I'll cry!

★ ★ ★

I wonder what it will actually be like when I move out of home. Obviously, I've already got my dream home planned out in my head but I haven't thought about how it will actually work. Like, who is going to cook for me? Is it acceptable to eat Nando's every night of the week? And how does a washing machine work?

★ ★ ★

December 24th

Hello, ridiculous Christmas pyjamas (Mum's gone above and beyond this year. These have got penguins <and> snowmen on them).

Hello, world's most comfortable sofa.

Hello, house covered in so many decorations it's hard to see the walls/ceilings/anything.

Hello, Christmas tree that's got the same fairy on top we've had since I was a baby.

Hello, Bella. And hello, Bella's miniature Christmas scarf.

And my god, hello family. How I've missed you. How I've missed <this>.

I'm back home in Brighton. I flew into Gatwick yesterday, and I got that really weird post-holiday thing. You know when you feel like home has changed so much? Only this time I've been away for almost a year. And I swear, I feel like a different person. It's been a massive adventure and I had such a crazy, funny, unexpected, amazing and, let's face it, pretty educational time.

My parents picked me up from the airport, and it reminded me of the arrivals scene in Love Actually *(my mum is obsessed with that film). It was so emotional, and once my parents started hugging me, I didn't think they were ever going to let me go.*

As we drove home, I wanted to look at every single little thing out of the window to see if it was how I remembered it. And it was. It was also absolutely freezing, which is something I'd forgotten about! I didn't take a coat to LA with me – even though it can get chilly in the evenings sometimes – and the hoodie I was wearing <definitely> wasn't made for the British winter.

I sat in the back of the car while Mum and Dad asked me loads of questions, and I felt like a little kid again. I've been standing on my own two feet for so long and being properly independent, so I'd felt like a real grown-up in some ways. But it's funny how the minute you're back in your parents' company, you revert to being their 'little girl'. And it feels really nice.

I got homesick a lot while I was in America, but it's only now I'm back that I realize how much and how many things I've missed. Even the familiar smell of my dad's car air freshener and his terrible, terrible jokes made me smile.

I went to LA thinking the pavements were paved with gold (which to be fair, they basically were, on the Walk of Fame). I thought what was over there was so much better than over here. It may be a lot sunnier and have better trees (I'll miss those palms) but, really, you take your attitude with you wherever you go. And as long as you're happy, you can be happy pretty much anywhere.

I learnt so much in such a short space of time.

I learnt that LA is a place of huge opportunity, but you also have to be tough and learn to deal with rejection pretty quickly.

I learnt that TuBot is a <massive> idiot, but I also kinda feel a bit sorry for him.

I learnt that sometimes when someone lets you down, they might actually be doing you a big favour. What happened with Ryan was horrible, but it showed me how quickly I can fight back. And that I always come back a little bit wiser, and a lot stronger.

I learnt that you have to take the crazy world of showbiz with a pinch of salt and know that for every one audition, there are a million girls who want it as badly as you do. And judging by the auditions I went along to, some of them are probably willing to step over you to get it.

I also learnt that I love YouTube more than ever. It gave me the opportunity to stay connected with home via my subscribers, who are such a big part of my life.The most important thing in the world to me is that I'm authentic, and YouTube gives me the opportunity to be that. My videos may not be perfect, but they're me. And I've realized just how much I like being me.

Vlogging gives me a chance to be exactly who I am, and I know for sure now that I am <enough>. Not film star Saffron, not world-famous Saffron, just . . . Saffron.

Even though I'm moving back to Brighton for now, Steve has asked if he can stay on as my agent. And I've said yes. Hilarious, right? But believe it or not, compared to the horror stories I heard while I was in Hollywood, he's one of the good ones! I'll totally still go up for auditions (luckily loads are done over Skype these days). But I'll make sure I find out exactly what I'm trying out for before I agree to them.

Just before I left LA, I felt like I should kind of wrap things up (you know, so I've got closure, as the Americas say). So I took a deep breath and I checked out ToolBot's YouTube channel. And crazily, I now have more subscribers than him. It seems like everyone has got a bit sick and tired of him making other people look stupid to get views, and they've jumped ship.

I never, ever take pleasure in other people's misery because I think it's one of the worst things you can do. But after embarrassing me, Toolbot ended up doing all sorts of other mean things. He catfished this one girl, so when she turned up to a date expecting to meet a 'guy' she'd been chatting to on WhatsApp, he jumped out and gunged her (sigh). Then he put all the WhatsApp conversations up online to add to her humiliation. Next, he posted a really unflattering photo of his ex-girlfriend all over their neighbourhood, and then filmed her as she ran around desperately trying to take them all down.

I mean, the guy isn't funny, he's <mean>.

I had a pretty rough time after the whole kiss thing, but I always try to take the positives from situations, and I guess it gave me a good story to tell (especially now I can laugh about it).

I hope ToolBot is okay and that he finds a way to get stats that doesn't involve making other people look and feel bad. Maybe this will be a big life lesson for him? 🙏. Or maybe . . . <not>.

Christmas with my family is the best thing <ever>. Seriously. I like it even more than shopping. And, as you know, I love shopping <a lot>.

As soon as December 1st comes, we put our tree and decorations up and we're good to go. It's a countdown until the big day, and the whole family will be really excited.

I write my first Christmas list in October or November, but I have to keep changing it because I always think of new things I'd like.

We always go out for dinner on Christmas Eve, because it's my dad's birthday, so that's such a nice way to build up to the big day. Then I'll go and pick holly to put on the table, which has become a real tradition. After that, we sit down and watch a Christmas movie together. I love *The Polar*

Express, but *Elf* is my favourite film of all time. I have no idea how many times I've seen it now, but I still laugh in all the same parts.

Christmas music is the best thing ever too. I love Destiny's Child's '8 Days of Christmas', and of course all the really brilliant cheesy songs like 'Merry Christmas, Everyone' and 'Jingle Bells'. My dad always ends up singing along and that's agony, so we turn it up so we can't hear it, meaning it gets louder and louder as time goes on.

Christmas Day is amazing in our house. There are always so many of us because all the family come over. There are usually about twenty people or so, which is a lot of people to fit around a table. Our record is twenty-four. Everyone sits so close together we're virtually on each other's laps. It's just as well we get on so well.

I wish I could say I help out with cooking the Christmas dinner but I <so> don't. In my defence, I'm usually busy because I have to film my 'What I got for Christmas' video actually <on> Christmas day. I never have a day off. But I honestly don't mind. It's so worth it.

My granddad is obsessed with Christmas, and Nan and Granddad's house is like *National Lampoon's Christmas Vacation* by the time they've finished decorating it (if you've never seen it, Google it. It's one of the best films ever). I feel bad for anyone else who lives in the Brighton area, because

I can't see how there are any decorations left to buy once they've hit the shops.

I get amazing presents and I've never been disappointed. Spoilt! I make a Christmas list every year, and my mum will use it as inspiration and then get me something I'll like even more. My mum has got really cool taste, so I never have that awful panic, thinking she'll buy me something awful and I'll have to pretend to like it. I've never been given a minging present and then had to do a happy face.

The best present I ever got was Katy Perry concert tickets. I cried my eyes out. Basically, I was all about Justin Bieber for ages, and then I suddenly became obsessed with Katy Perry after watching her movie (I'd recommend it, it's amazing). It's all about how she struggled when she first started out and she got bullied, so whenever I was having a hard time I'd think about what she went through to get where she is. I really look up to her as a person, and it helped when things were hard in the band. I'd think, 'If Katy Perry can go through everything she did and still be massively strong and successful, so can I.' I'd never looked up to someone like that before. I'd obsessed over Justin because of what he looked like, but with Katy, she was a massive inspiration and she really motivated me.

Mum had told me the tickets had sold out, so there was no way of getting them, and I was disappointed, but that's just the way it was and I had to suck it up.

I remember getting this envelope for Christmas, and when I opened it and saw the tickets, I was so shocked and I could not stop crying. Then, when I went to the concert, I cried all over again. I was shaking and everything. I'm not a 'fan' as such now, but she's still a huge role model for me.

I also got a laptop for Christmas one year, and that changed my life. I used to have to share my mum's old laptop and use it to try and edit my videos, and it was so slow, it would take foreeeever. When I got my own, it was the best thing ever. I was like, 'Hallelujah! It's a new me!' It was amazing.

Here's a bit about my last two Christmases, both of which I loved

The year before last, I woke up really early at, like, 2.46am, and then I kept waking up at the same time every hour after that. I was so tired! I went and woke everyone up, because I couldn't wait for the day to start. I woke Casey and Nicole up first, and they were not impressed.

Jed was next, and I honestly didn't think he'd get up. But then I mentioned the magic word – presents. Casey woke poor Jordan up by jumping on him, and then it was Mum and Dad's turn.

When we went downstairs, we all had our stockings laid out, and the carrot and the mince pie we left out for Santa had been half-eaten. So cute.

We all got such amazing presents. Casey bought Nicole some Louboutins and she straight up cried. I don't think she could believe it. It was such a lovely reaction, and I couldn't blame her. I would cry at Louboutins too.

Dad made us some breakfast (while wearing his elf slippers, of course), and then I got dressed before the family started arriving. My little cousin Ivy-Mae sang 'Whoops-a-Daisy-Angel' with her new pink Christmas guitar, and I swear my heart actually nearly melted.

Poor Jordan fell asleep, so we drew on him with pen and when he woke up, he rubbed his face, and it went everywhere. We laughed so much, and we finished the day by playing charades (a Christmas essential).

It was such an incredible and manic day. We all wore ridiculous festive hats, I got some spoons in a cracker (er, yay) and my nan posed for a selfie with me. #Christmasgoals

It was perfect.

Christmas 2016 was every bit as brilliant, but also a bit different because Casey and Nicole were in Brazil seeing Nicole's family, so it was just the five of us.

The first half an hour was all about our miniature sacks and <presents!> One of the first things I opened was a light-up mirror, which I'd wanted for, like, ever.

Next, it was time to put on some Christmas music and open our main presents. I also helped Bella open hers, and she got a very cool gold hat, which I <think> she liked. It can be kinda hard to tell with her sometimes.

I bought my mum the most beautiful bag. It was <insane>, and of course I wanted to keep it for myself.

But I got totally spoilt too. As always. In fact, we got so many presents it took us forever to open them, so we were still in our pyjamas by the time our family arrived.

We ate! We sang! We played pie face! I filmed and edited videos! And then I fell asleep. Obviously.

Boxing Day always feels a little bit sad because Christmas is done and dusted, but we still have a lovely time, and it was the same last year. I always hate the fact that Christmas is over again. I'm not kidding, I already start looking forward to the next one to make myself feel better.

I always think I'm going to relax over Christmas and sleep loads, but I end up planning things and seeing my mates, and last year I spent ages doing make-up looks and making videos.

The whole of Christmas week is one of those times that I can look back on, like, a week later, and those days will already feel like amazing memories.

December 25th – Christmas Day

It's heeeeeeeeeere! I've got antlers on, I'm opening presents and I could not be happier. Seriously, even if Zac Efron and Brooklyn Beckham merged into one person and walked through the door and proposed to me, I don't think I could smile any more than I am right now. This is basically what life is all about.

I can't imagine what it would be like if I was back in LA having Christmas in the sun. I love the fact that it's so cold in the UK and I can put on my onesie and feel at peace with the world. I can look as terrible as I like, and no one cares. And everyone is being so <nice> to me. Apart from Jed, who got over the excitement of me being home in, like, two seconds, and is now spending most of the time joking about how much he <didn't> miss me.

I was hoping that after being away for so long, Jed would magically agree to be in one of my videos. Especially as I spotted that he'd appeared in one of Casey's while I was away. I was so shocked! But when I asked? Forget it. Unless I agreed to give up for my bedroom for him (which, amazingly, he hadn't moved into while I was away).

Leonie messaged me earlier to say Happy Christmas, and it was so good to hear from her. I had a moment of 'Do I wish

I was still over there?' but I know I'm right where I should be. Leonie also showed me what she got for Christmas – a ticket to England! She's coming to visit! I can't wait to show her around so she can see all the places I've been talking about for <so> long. I know Brighton Pier won't be quite as glamorous as Long Island, but I think she'll love how kitsch it is. She may even get some inspo for her collection. Her clothing range is really taking off. Hailey Baldwin wore one of her dresses to a premiere recently, and after that things started to go a bit nuts.

Beth may also be coming over next year. She's hoping to start doing some make-up work over here, and she's been offered representation by this really great agency. So if things come off, she could be jetting between LA and London, which means I'll get to see her loads. Yaaaaaaay! Life is gooooooood!

Oh, and did I mention I got a secret Santa gift from someone who genuinely is, like, totally secret? It was dropped off outside my house on Christmas Eve and it was the cutest box of presents.

It contained a really beautiful Jo Malone candle, some chocolate raisins (that I will try not to get stuck in my teeth), a unicorn mug, some really cosy slippers and a bottle of Jimmy Choo perfume.

It must be from someone who knows me really well, but I

have no idea who. I'm really looking forward to finding out, though. There is nothing more exciting than a bit of Christmas romance.

★ ★ ★

I really, really hope you've enjoyed reading this book. I've had so much fun writing it, and I've loved creating my (slightly crazy) fantasy life.

I could have made it totally perfect and got the guy / become a multi-millionaire / conquered the world. But let's face it, that wouldn't have been very me. All the ideas came from inside my head, and basically everything in there is a little bit ridiculous. I had so much fun (sort of) living in LA, hanging out in cool places and meeting incredible people. But actually it made me realize something. Make-believe lives are great, and it's so important to have dreams and goals. But this normal, everyday reality stuff with my crazy family? That's pretty amazing too.

ACKNOWLEDGEMENTS

Firstly, I want to say that I'm so grateful to have such amazing people in my life. I've got a few thank yous, so here goes. . .

A huge thank you to Jordan Paramor for your patience, and for sitting and listening to my strange, crazy and sometimes sad stories for hours on end, and for really getting me. Without you this book wouldn't be as fab as it is.

Thanks so much to everyone at Hodder, especially Briony Gowlett, for believing I was interesting enough to write a book about in the first place, and for being so enthusiastic about it every step of the way.

A big, big thank you to my managers Jonathan Poole and Kate Lovett and the rest of the Red Hare team for always believing in me and pushing me forward.

Mum, thank you for everything. I don't believe my appreciation for you is always as clear as it could be, so this is a thank you from the bottom of my heart for being the best mum ever. You're the one person I can always count on to get me through my days, and you're always right there by my side throughout everything. You believed in me even before I believed in myself, and I know you'll always have my back whatever happens. I don't believe this YouTube dream would have even been possible if you weren't a part of it. I really don't know what I would do without you, so the biggest thank of all goes to you.

And, of course, my brilliant dad. Your constant flow of silly (yet hilarious) video ideas come in very useful, even though I find it hard to admit sometimes. Your zest for life and enthusiasm brightens up every single day. I don't know where I'd be without your constant belief in me, pushing me to achieve my dreams and encouraging me to believe I can do anything I want to. Thank you for everything.

I also want to thank the rest of my incredible family for being so tolerant when you have a camera shoved in your faces at every opportunity, and for being as excited about this book as I am.

And last, but certainly not least, I want to thank all of you guys for your continued support. You are such a massive part of my journey. It's my dream to meet every single one of you one day and thank you personally. Here's to lots more exciting times in the future!